What People Are Saying About Patrice Bisiot

Style Interventionist

"Patrice is the first person who has been able to clearly diagnose, demonstrate and advise me on how to align my look with my message through simple but precise changes. I would highly recommend Patrice for no-nonsense coaching on how to make a greater impact on the people in your life."

— Marcus Zacco – Business Developer

"Patrice Bisiot's Image Impact consultation was a complete game-changer. I thought my Image was polished and professional—but five minutes with Patrice changed my thinking. What a shock! My business mission was (and is) to help entrepreneurs keep pace with change by moving them in new directions for the future. I didn't realize—until Patrice came along—that my look was itself out of date and creating a barrier to me selling the future and change. Why would clients believe I could help them move forward when I still looked like the past? Now, however, I walk into a room and the way I look shows clients I am with the times and not afraid to go to the edge. I often close the deal in one meeting. My business has doubled in 18 months! I am living proof that Image has a direct Impact on the success of your business."

— Cindy Brown – Founding Partner,
Brown Welch Mehta LLP

"With his knowledge, compassion, and wisdom, Patrice Bisiot transformed my career and my life. I was in a down-turn emotionally, personally, and professionally. It never occurred to me that how I packaged myself (hair, clothes, subtle touches, etc.) could make a difference. But after Patrice performed a style intervention, my career took off…and my personal life along with it!"

— Rick Henderson – Private Equity Banker

"Patrice has worked with me for 20 years, navigating me through celebrity Award Shows and galas from Cannes to Sundance to Beverly Hills. We've collaborated on different looks—from sharp and edgy to playful to Old Hollywood. And every time, the look is perfect for what I want to say. Bravo Patrice!"

— Christine King – Brand Strategist,
TMG International

"Patrice has helped me to understand that "image" is really about the way people respond to you. Thank you Patrice for your invaluable knowledge and guidance! You rock!"

— Sharon Cohen – Music Executive

"Patrice was instrumental in helping me uncover and embrace my personal brand. Prior to Patrice, shopping for clothes, doing my hair, or putting my style together were dictated by my mood that day and not the image I wanted to project. Patrice has guided me through the process of discovering a look that is truly my own so now, when meeting people, I am impactful and influential."

— Seanlai – Sensual Behaviorist & Host,
Two Wild Orchids

“I feel beautiful, powerful, positive, and strong—essential feelings I could never have achieved without Patrice’s expert guidance. Our conversation started ten years ago when Patrice helped me realize I was using my hair as ARMOR (and not in a good way either). Since then, Patrice’s talent and vision have carried me through to my own brand awareness. I love collaborating with him on each new look—each time, a complete success!”

— Stacey Callahan – Rue 57, General Manager

“Patrice has been my stylist and more importantly my friend. It is in large part because of him that I have learned the importance of self-care and presentation. As I’ve transitioned into some of the most important roles of my life—wife, professional, mother—Patrice has helped me take on those roles with confidence and strength.”

— Alejandra Crowe – Vice President,
Financial Institution

“When Patrice helped me realize that my look—my hair in particular—was working against me, we created a new style that changed everything. After taking his instructions and picture examples to my hairstylist, I instantly felt the impact and the confidence within it. Patrice helped me align all the elements of my appearance to match my brand and message.”

— Lucas Robok – Keynote Speaker,
Consultant, Bestselling Author

"I have been Patrice's client and friend for 20 years. Every three weeks, from whatever city he may be working in, he does his magic with my appearance. I come out looking twenty years younger! I have been an ardent student of his first book, *Mind Your Hair*. He has vast knowledge of how males and females should present themselves whether it be for meetings, employment, or social occasions. Patrice knows hair and dress inside-out. I truly value his expertise."

—Martin Schubert – CEO,
European InterAmerican Finance Corp.

"I had not changed my look since college. Just the thought of changing it was terrifying! Then Patrice came along and challenged me to a transformation! Well…the reactions from those around me were immediate! Suddenly, my external appearance reflected the confidence and vitality I always wanted to project. I've since learned how important it is to let your appearance grow with you. It's so great to feel confident and beautiful and to let my personality shine through. Patrice, I am grateful for your artistry and friendship!"

—Sabine Hesse – MD FACS

MIND YOUR IMPACT

BUILD
YOUR BRAND

MAXIMIZE
YOUR INFLUENCE

EMPOWER
YOUR LIFE

PATRICE BISIOT

STYLE INTERVENTIONIST

AVIVA PUBLISHING

New York

Address all inquiries to:
Patrice Bisiot
info@talktoPatrice.com
ImageImpactIndex.com

ISBN: 978-1-950241-75-0 paperback
ISBN: 978-1-950241-76-7 hardcover

Library of Congress Control Number: 2021919334
First paperback edition June 2021

Aviva Publishing
Lake Placid, NY 12946
518.523.1320
www.avivapubs.com

Dedication

I dedicate this second book to
my amazing support group and community.

Acknowledgments

FIRST TO MY MOM, COLETTE, BIGGEST FAN AND SUPPORTER, who listened to me daily about my greatest victories and my frustrations…

To my sister Jenny who always believes in me and my dreams.

To Lorraine Garnett, my editor, coach, teacher and more. She helped understanding my vision, mission and purpose, page after page, extracting all this data in my brain to create the most incredible content and make this book a Branding Bible for generations to come...

And last but not least, ALL of You, my friends, my support group, my loving community. Throughout the years with your messages, your response to my weekly posts, your encouragement without which I couldn't be here right now. I am SO grateful for your Love.

Contents

Preface

FROM CHILDHOOD I POSSESSED A GIFT. I could perceive things, situations and people "differently." I could "see" their life in an instant—with just that first glance at them. I could "see" a better version of people. I could "see" the secrets they were trying to cover up. I could "see" the pain and insecurity. I could "see" them uncovered and find that one tweak to *change everything* for them.

I also knew my gift was sent to me to make a difference in the world. My mission was to use this artistic gift to dramatically improve the lives of others. This book is the fulfillment of that mission.

This book is not a memoir. This book explains my gift and illustrates the powerful impact your image makes not only on the world, but most importantly, on you! I use real life examples of my clients to show you ONLY one tiny change—mascara, jeans, shoes—can alter the course of your life. Sound dramatic? Well, the results certainly are dramatic.

This book is proof that anyone, from the CEO of a multinational company to people like you, can finally discover ONLY ONE THING in your appearance does change everything in your life. Most people go a lifetime knowing they are just one tweak away from the life they know they deserve. I am giving you the secret of that tweak!

This book represents many, many years of experience on the red carpet, on television, and preparing for press events with celebrities, global leaders, thought provokers, and entrepreneurs. It represents years and years of collecting data to understand how to align emotions with image. Gathering data points on how to align what you wear and how you think you look to how you feel.

I have taken all of this knowledge and put it into a simple coaching program. This process will help you to communicate your message with just your "look" every time you step out of your house. We will develop Your Brand—Your Signature—Your Image—Your Impact.

You are about to understand the power of appearance, the psychology of Image and its Impact, not just on yourself, but on the world at large. A simple step-by-step process, one chapter at a time, where I changed ONE thing from someone's appearance and turned their whole life around! Literally.

When you walk into a room, you have but a microsecond (the 5 second rule is just an urban myth), to make a life lasting impact. There is no re-do, no second chance. The job is done in that moment and that moment alone. You show up. The way you look right here, right now tells the world your life story. Say it precisely. Say it positively. Say it powerfully.

Time to *regain your power*. Time to *be remembered*. Time to *create your brand*.

Let's go!

CHAPTER 1

Through New Eyes

IT WAS A TINY CHANGE. Something you would measure in micrometers; it changed my mother's sense of self . . . and started me on my life's journey.

I was eleven when I discovered the butterfly effect. Make a tiny change in a tiny detail and someone's world is upended. In my case, the tiny change was in my mother's appearance, and the change was my idea.

I grew up in France's Loire Valley in a town known as "the Venice of the Gâtinais." I was surrounded by picture-postcard views—waterways flanked by ancient houses, grand mansions, exotic gardens, a castle dating back to the

12th Century. Although we didn't have smart phones with cameras then (this was still the 20th Century), I had a photographic visual imagination. I would take snapshots using just my mind's eye, then I'd mentally "photoshop" them. I'd swap out colors, repaint window trims, if an ancient structure needed cleaning—and many of them did—in my mind I would do the job.

I remember seeing a row of stone houses along the banks of la Rivière le Loing. The stones were covered with grime, centuries of it, and the water reflected their murky greyness. The scene, I decided, needed help badly. I went to work visualizing what it would look like with the stones restored to their original luster. It was definitely an improvement, yet it still needed a splash of color. In the background I superimposed a haze of purple lavender, an image I cheerfully borrowed from les jardins du Château de Montargis.

Looking back, I believe I did this to bring harmony into my less than harmonious childhood. I was attempting to numb myself to bullies at school and to my father's vile temper. To outsiders watching me who didn't know this, I was just a kid who stared a lot. They'd catch me staring off into space or, worse, staring at people, as my habit of mental "photo editing" wasn't just limited to scenery.

There was a woman at our post office with the most

beautifully arched eyebrows that she hid under heavy bangs. I remember her confronting me, demanding to know why I was looking at her and if there was something in her hair. I was giving her an imaginary bang trim and I couldn't tell her that.

* * *

"Your eyes are like laser beams, you read people to the depths of their souls." Those were my mother's words. My mother had her own ideas about my habit of staring at people. To her, it was a rare and special gift. It also was a practical gift, and she put it to immediate and practical use.

My mother was a stay-at-home mom who took care of four children, a six-bedroom house, a growing brood of rescue animals, and a demanding husband. On those rare and much-anticipated occasions of a family gathering or dinner out, she loved dressing up for it. To her it was a restoring ritual. She would retreat to her private sanctuary, her dressing area in their bedroom and then to the bathroom mirror.

My mother was petite, had a tiny waist, and instinctively understood her personal look and how to give it the best light. Skirts not too long, not too short, colors just bright enough yet never too bright. There was no money for real jewels, but the yellow-gold of her costume jewelry was just the right yellow-gold, not too shiny just shiny enough. My mother had an eye for elegance—alas, only a shoestring budget. The challenge was to make the same few garments always look new and surprising.

That's where my "photoshop" brain came in.

I was nine when my mother first asked me for help putting her outfits together. I remember sitting in rapt attention, watching each variation as we found new ways to make a stylish statement. My mother's dressing area was well mirrored except she didn't always trust what she saw. This is how I became my mother's other mirror, observing, describing, giving her my thumbs up or thumbs down, and feeling very grown up and important.

After my mother was fully dressed, scarf and pin just so, she would emerge from the bathroom and tiptoe into the room where my father's eyes were glued to the TV screen. My father was a no-nonsense, macho type whose identity was tied to his professional achievements as a scientist and mathematician and to his championship in amateur boxing.

My dressed-up mother would wait for my father to view the outfit we created. She would wait and wait. All the while he would pretend not to see her. Make a big show of having better things to do.

A man is supposed to compliment his wife when she

goes to the trouble to make herself pretty. I was a kid and I knew it, I believe even cavemen knew it. My father went out of his way to deny my mother what she longed for.

It's easy to say someone ought to feel good about themselves and not need outside reassurance. My mother didn't have that kind of mettle. To her, compliments were like a shot of endorphin, and I was determined she should have them. This is where my mother and I came to a difference of opinion. As I said, my mother didn't always trust what she saw in the mirror. On one point she was certain: she could never be beautiful. Pleasant-looking, yes, even pretty. Elegant, absolutely. Beautiful? Don't even try. Like many people, my mother had a least favorite feature. Her "worst" feature happened to be her eyes. They protruded a little more than normal, a remnant of a one-time thyroid condition. In my mother's opinion, her eyes looked "buggy." In my opinion, they were hidden gems.

What my mother didn't see, what I saw, was she had two different faces. One was the face she saw in the mirror, always scowling at her hated eyes. In years to come, on photoshoots with my once-idolized supermodels, I would watch them scowl at their mirrors much as my mother did. I've come to believe it is universal to focus on the thing we dislike most, and this makes us less attractive than we normally are.

My mother's second face was one she never saw. This was the loving face I saw when she turned and looked at me. This face was smiling. But there was also another face—the one I created on the screen in my mind and wanted to create in actuality. My mother had pale blonde lashes, which made them almost invisible. Unless you were up close, her eyes really did seem to vanish. My mother routinely wore lipstick and powder, but when I told her she should wear mascara, she became strangely obstinate. I believe she wanted her eyes to vanish.

Have you ever been shopping and watched a kid bugging a parent to buy something? I was eleven and we were shopping at the market and, as usual, I wandered off. Only this time I discovered the cosmetics aisle. Imagine seeing a lovely French housewife accompanied by her pubescent son and he's bugging her to buy mascara. My mother had no choice but to give in, stash it away in the back of a drawer, and forget she had it.

But I knew it was there...

Some time later when my mother was dressing, I saw her self-confidence was particularly low.

"Maybe I need a different scarf... maybe I should tie it sideways... maybe a necklace... maybe..."

I could feel her emotional turmoil. I sat her down on the edge of the bathtub, the mascara wand was already in my hand. My instinct told me she really needed what I was about to do.

I had imagined this moment already in my mind. My movements were confident and steady. Holding the wand at just the right angle, I directed it toward her eye. My mother flinched and dodged me. I waited a moment, tried again, and once again she flinched. Blink reflexes are a problem even for the very top makeup artists. I know this now, but I didn't then. I kept trying, and she kept flinching—until she pulled the wand from my hand.

Then my mother surprised me, she applied the mascara herself. Her movements were halting and awkward at first, it was obvious she hadn't done this before. Nonetheless, she managed. It was amazing to watch as her once hidden feature morphed into view. Here's the thing—my mother's "worst" feature became her most beautiful. I'd been on school field trips to Paris's le Musée d'Orsay where I saw amazing art treasures and learned they too were seen as "ugly."

In those first few moments of my mother's transformation when I saw her from over her shoulder, her eyes actually took my breath away. I think they took her breath away too.

"Let's show my father," I said. Normally, I'd steer clear of these viewings where my father would go out of his way to show his wife how much she didn't matter. But this time I couldn't wait.

My father was, as usual, in front of the TV. Whatever he was watching must have been exciting, as I heard loud cheers coming from the set. This time, nothing on the screen could keep him from noticing his wife's transformation. He actually jumped up from his armchair.

Then he uttered the following words, which to this day are etched in my brain: *"C'est quoi ça? Un vrai maquillage de catin! On dirait que tu travailles au coin de la rue!"* In English they are: "What's this? A true makeup whore! Looks like you work on a street corner!"

There's no way I can describe my initial reaction. I remember noticing my younger siblings who'd been in the room all the time. They stopped playing and stood in stunned silence. I don't think they understood the words, but they knew it was bad.

Then I saw my mother crying. The tears had already liquified the mascara and it was running down her cheeks. I said what I could to defend her—I was, after all, responsible. Arguing with my father was futile. To him, the purpose of a woman's beauty was to attract a husband. Once accomplished, beauty was useless. If that beauty boosted a woman's sense of self... well, women have to be kept in their place.

Sadly, my mother retreated to the safety of unremarkable-looking eyes. But the lift she'd gotten from seeing them otherwise, even though only momentary, planted a seed in her mind. I'd catch her trying to touch her lashes with just the minutest amount of color, and then wipe most of it off.

"Put on more, you look beautiful," I'd tell her. She'd hesitate, look at herself again, then something inside would stop her.

Then one day, some time afterwards, my mother and I were preparing for an afternoon of errands and window shopping. It would just be the two of us, my father wasn't around. On a whim, my mother decided to go out in public with fully mascaraed lashes. She would give her "new face" a trial run. Feeling like naughty children whose parents had left them on their own, mother and I strolled forth. We strolled along la rue Dorée, a street famous for its boutiques and cafés. We peered into elegant boutique windows and stopped for a moment by a shop we knew well. When we were about to move on, the shopkeeper ran out after us. What did he want?

Turns out he'd caught a glimpse of my mother and couldn't get over how well she looked. He just had to tell her. There are moments when our brains need to re-boot. For my mother, this was one of them. She had just been admired and complimented—which was what she wanted most—and she was having a hard time accepting it. Was the shopkeeper for real? Was he making fun of her? Although she didn't say these things out loud, I knew what my mother was thinking. We were in front of another shop a few moments later. This time a saleswoman waved us in. She wanted to know if my mother had colored her hair. And so it went—all up and down la rue Dorée, people who knew us even slightly bestowed my mother with praise and admiration. The world seemed to be smiling that day.

* * *

Honk . . . honk . . . honk . . . honk!

My father was in the car having a mini temper tantrum and taking it out on his horn. My sister and brothers were in the back seat, they didn't like waiting either. I had butterflies in my stomach.

My mother sat on the edge of the bathtub so I could render my final touches. Her lashes were already fully coated, and I was coloring her eyelids a shimmering, iridescent green.

When the two stragglers finally piled into the car, my father was too preoccupied with his honking to notice anything different. Then during the drive, when he finally did notice, it was too late to do anything about it, so all he could do was roll his eyes.

The family gathering was at my grandmother's, the grandmother on my mother's side. I waited with my mother for the others to go in first—I wanted this to be a grand entrance. Flawless alabaster skin—never exposed to the sun—and a sweet, winning smile had always been my mother's trademark, but now she had the wow factor—big, exotic, fascinating eyes. My mother hadn't processed her rue Dorée experience. Now she was about to be overwhelmed. Aunts, great-aunts, uncles, cousins . . . the flow of admiration was heart-warming. Sweetest of all was when my mother's own mother, my grandmother, greeted her daughter with tears in her eyes, seeing the pretty daughter she hadn't seen in a very long time.

Thus went an important turning point in my mother's journey toward self-worth. In time, she would be happily single, and she would wear, or not wear, whatever pleased her. Changes often incubate on the inside before they become apparent—so it would be with my mother—one small change on the outside and enormous change on the inside!

What is your tiny change on the outside that will make a big shift on the inside? Do you know? Go in front of the mirror, stand and take a long look at yourself. Look at every part. What do you avoid? Where do you stare? What do you see? Give it words.

Embrace your reflection and answer these questions. What is your most powerful feature? How do you cherish it? How do you incorporate it in your appearance? How does it empower you? How can it change your journey?

When I answered these questions, my own journey to create the life of my dreams began.

CHAPTER 2

Transformation

I KNOW PEOPLE WHO BUILD UP THEIR CONFIDENCE by reciting affirmations. I was wearing mine.

It started with a mood board—a collage of pictures I gathered from my grandmother's copies of *Pointe de Vue Images du Monde* (France's last word on celebrities and royals) and my mother's copies of *Vogue*. No, I didn't actually cut up their magazines—the collage lived in my imagination where it became my secret friend.

I was an awkward kid, skinny, puny, scared of my own shadow and of the school roughnecks who made me their target. In my imagination, I could feast my eyes on their betters—like my first love, Princess Caroline and her father, Prince Rainier. There was a baby-faced chubby kid at school who used to bully me on the playground. Pinned flat under him, I would look up, and while his lips were saying the worst things, I'd be thinking how his haircut was horrible. Prince Rainier never would have let his hair look like that!

I told you I used to help my mother choose clothes and put on makeup—I have vivid memories of looking over her shoulder and seeing what she saw in the mirror. But I left out an important detail: Although we were always in front of mirrors, and I always saw my mother in them—I never saw myself.

I made sure not to. I knew just where to sit, where to stand, exactly how to angle my body so I wouldn't have to see my reflection. Because if I saw it, even for a moment, I would have an awful sinking feeling and wish the ground would open up and swallow me.

I remember getting a haircut once and looking down at my feet the whole time—anything to avoid the dreaded mirror. A frustrated hairstylist kept asking me to "Please, lift your head up!"

Problem was, I felt small on the inside. What I saw in the mirror was a reflection of how I felt. If I were to revisit my childhood now, as an outside observer, I would see a hunched over kid who hugged his shoulders and wore clothes so big he got lost in them. No wonder I attracted bullies—I made myself a target!

My mother, meanwhile, remained blissfully unaware. I would rather have died than let her see me as anything other than her protector and champion. In private, I wished I could shed my skin. In private, I licked my wounds from being bullied and beaten. Still, I was my mother's hero—it kept me going. It was what I lived for and I was willing to pay the price for it.

My father, as I told you, was a macho type—a boxer, scientist, mathematician, and stickler for traditional "gender lanes." Since I was my mother's fashion collaborator, I clearly had stepped out of mine. If I tell you my father couldn't handle having me for a son, that would be an understatement.

I remember cramming for a math test once. One of the equations just didn't make sense to me. I had two options: risk going in unprepared for the test or risk facing the wrath of my mathematician father (who regarded math prowess as a measure of manliness). I chose the wrath.

Just as I feared, my father greeted me with curses and insults—and he used a certain French word, the meaning of which I didn't understand. I tried very hard to hear what he was saying (since his rant did include a few crumbs of math wisdom), but my brain transformed my father's words into a stream of meaningless static.

Next thing I knew, his bare-knuckled punches were hammering both sides of my head. The pain was excruciating. To keep from crying, I filled my eyes with immediate visual input. I focused on his cuffs, I thought they were too high; on his back pockets, they were placed too low; and on his slicked-back black hair, it looked like a helmet. I noticed his nails were short and clean, his silver wrist bracelet was scratched and the sheen was dull.

The following morning, I ached all over, yet somehow, I made it to school. I did not do well on my math test and to this day, I struggle with a mental block toward all things numerical or technical.

* * *

"Un coiffeur?"

"Un coiffeur!"

"Coiffeur" is French for "hairstylist." From the way my school counselor hissed the word, you'd think it was a profanity.

I was fifteen and accompanied by both parents. We had been summoned to my school counselor's office to discuss why I was dropping out. I was, after all, the son of a PhD, I had a "gifted" IQ, and, except in math, I was an

"A" student. My counselor said I was throwing my life away. I told him I would be famous and rich. He said I was dreaming.

My decision to go to beauty school was, in fact, a well thought out plan as a means of creating my dream life. Specifically, it came from a common thread I noticed in celebrity photographs—everyone always had perfect hair! From this detail, I surmised the invisible presence of *un coiffeur* always lurking just outside the picture frame. I wanted to be that presence.

I will paraphrase in English what I said next, because what came out of me was startling: "I don't want to be ordinary. You'll see . . . I'll be famous! I'll travel the world. . . . I'll be in magazines. . . . People will recognize me. . . . I'll be somebody. . . ."

My mother smiled sweetly as I spoke; my school counselor grimaced and rolled his eyes; my father shrugged (he'd long since given up on me); and I felt a surge of excitement like nothing I'd ever experienced before.

Until then, my dream lived inside me, locked away deep in my mind where no one could take it away. When I blurted it out—my voice became fuller; I stood taller; I'd taken a stand for myself. With all my daytime bravado, later that night, in my private darkness, I asked myself, *Who am I kidding?*

Not long before, I had been walking down the street when I tried to approach a passerby to find out what time it was. I caught her eye; she looked right at me, and suddenly, I felt exposed. My body responded as if it were being eyed by a hungry tiger: cold sweat, shallow breathing, heart pounding—the works. I looked away, hoping to hide my face. I must have spoken in a whisper because the woman kept asking me to please repeat myself.

Sure, I could hobnob with celebrities in the privacy of my imagination, but in reality . . . well, reality was another universe.

* * *

I will refer to the lady in question as "Mme." As directress of l'Ecole Supérieure de Coiffure, arguably Paris' most prestigious beauty school (and by extension, the world's), Mme was a formidable presence.

Needless to say, she scared the bejesus out of me. In the very near future, Mme would jolt me out of my shell and into reality. Now I'm getting ahead of myself. . . .

At the end of week one, we were given practice mannequins. The mannequins were mounted in narrow workstations, and mounted in each workstation was my old nemesis—the mirror.

The idea was to get us used to seeing our work from

different angles. It wasn't enough just to see it in front of you; you had to see it the way your client did—in the mirror. A shock of realization came over me—mirrors are part of a hairstylist's world! When I had dreamed up my glorious future, I had somehow left the mirror part out! Now I realized why . . .

Every year, when I was little, my mother took me shopping for school clothes. I hated it. What I really hated was seeing myself. The kids at school hardly noticed me except to kick me around.

Is it because of how I look? I wondered.

The store mirror confirmed my thinking. Skinny arms, skinny shoulders, skinny legs, skinny everything. Nothing I tried on ever fit. Pants, especially, were a nightmare. When the waist was small enough for the pants to stay up, the legs barely reached my ankles. When the legs were long enough, the waist was enormous; without a tight belt, pants would fall off me.

Then there was a matronly sales woman who would dig fingers under my waistband, gather up the loose material, and exclaim, *"Tu es tellement maigre!" "Maigre"* is French for "skinny," and it stung me to the core. In the mirror, I saw this "meagre" kid in too-big trousers who looked like he was wearing a potato sack. So there I was, peering over my mannequin, seeing what she'd see if she were a living person. I slouched down low enough for the top of my head to be level with hers—anything to not see myself.

Meanwhile, a commotion had broken out around me. The workstations were only partly partitioned so I could see my classmates, and they could see me. I discovered I wasn't the only one who could be spooked by a mirror. In different ways, *everyone* was. Some tried to "fix" themselves (comb their hair, maybe squeeze a zit); a few made funny faces; still others assumed postures of exaggerated nonchalance, as if to say, "Mirror, I don't care what you think of me."

Mme, of course, took all of this in. Mme, I soon learned, had a way of seeing everything. I swear, she could see through walls. When she finally called the group to order, she delivered a powerful wake up call. To summarize Mme's message: It isn't enough to master your craft. It isn't enough even if you are great at it.... You have to *look* great doing it. You are onstage; your client is your audience. The mirror is someone watching you....

Fortunately, Mme's pronouncement came at the end of the day. I needed to escape; I needed to process. So I walked over to les Champs-Élysées where I could gaze unseen at the *soigné* set and dream of "someday" being one of them. The old comforting sense of peace again came over me, but this time I knew better: Dreaming about my "future" was one thing; facing it was another.

So next morning, I was back at school, facing my workstation, my mannequin, my mirror, and Mme's surprise visits. It takes repetition for new learning to stick, and Mme gave me plenty of it. I was treated to a royal tongue-lashing every time she caught me slouching. Until then, I had been unaware of my posture (I was too busy disliking myself for other things). Mme's zero tolerance for what she called my lack of "presentation" gave me something new to worry about.

It seems strange now, I was in a weird way comfortable with all my insecurity and baggage. It was familiar. It felt like me. Then fate pulled a fast one.

We were in the school commons room; it was a special day. A few of us, the very best and most deserving, would be given actual live clients, people who paid for our services. If your name was called, which was a big *if,* you had to walk the length of the commons, past your envious fellow students, and personally greet your client. I was there among my classmates, feeling I was nothing special, and, like the others, wondering who would be called.

Then I heard her. We all did. Mme called my name. My first thought was, *This is a joke! She's rubbing salt into my already wounded ego!* Nonetheless, I placed one foot in front of the other and began the longest walk of my life. Mme spoke again.

This time she pronounced me her "number-one student" and told the others to "follow Patrice's example." Want to talk about a rush? Lord have mercy, it was way past that! From my toes all the way up to my hair roots . . . to this day, I struggle to make sense of what I felt. My universe, all I had ever known, had suddenly been pulled out from under me. I was achieving my dream! I was creating my dream life! I was fulfilled!

How about you? Have you dared to follow your dream? What was your first turning point? Did it elevate your self-esteem or just heighten your fear? Are you choosing the fear of the unknown over the fear of regret?

Where do you need help stepping into the light of your dreams and making the *impact* you desire?

CHAPTER 3

What I Learned From a Makeover Gone Wrong

THE LAND OF OPPORTUNITY OR MISSED OPPORTUNITY?

There was a time in my life when the United States of America seemed more like never-never land than a country. A place inhabited by picture-perfect beings. This notion came from airbrushed photographs and what I saw on the silver screen. Later, I learned better. I remained fascinated by the idea of the USA and anything American.

At age eighteen, I moved from France to Miami—South Beach to be exact. Miami's South Beach section was cool, trendy, newly-renovated, and happening. For the hairstylists who flocked there from all over the world, it was like living in the Gold Rush days.

I think back on one of my first haircuts when I came to Miami. It was in a hospital for a girl of nineteen, a cancer patient. I washed her hair in the hospital sink (which was NOT designed for that purpose), then sat her down in the armchair by the bed and unfolded my cutting cape. She told me how lucky she felt to have enough hair for me to cut. I remember how she smiled after I had finished. Her smile was bigger than life. She promised she would thank me for it every single day. A simple task, a haircut, it was as if I had performed a miracle.

After that, I quickly acquired a following and a reputation. My monikers included, "Hair Whisperer," "Hair Michelangelo," "Stravinsky of the Scissor," and my favorite, "Edward Scissorhands." Along with my reputation, came photoshoots in the Caribbean, house calls in amazing mansions, interviews on TV and other media . . . I was riding a very high wave and I was riding high! Had I found my *impact* on the world?

Early one morning in Miami, I woke up suddenly from a dream. The dream was still vivid in my mind and in it I remembered hearing people talking and I sensed they were talking about me. When I listened closely, they told me I would leave a legacy. Then I woke up.

But the dream stayed with me.

Remembering it, I started thinking, if I am here to leave a legacy, what will it be?

I'd already made a difference in my mother's life, and certainly in my own. Both involved appearances. Could my purpose be to make the world better by making its inhabitants look better? It was, after all, what I was trained for.

Here is what else was on my mind: I was troubled by what I saw as a growing trend in media—the so-called "beauty makeover."

If you won a contest or were the "lucky" person chosen from a studio audience, they said they would restyle your hair. Just expecting a new hairstyle, the contestant found that their "makeover" changed *everything* not just hair. Why? Because audiences like seeing change, big change. What do you think happened afterward? Bliss? Loved the new look? Shock and despair? An unplanned change this drastic very seldom has a happy ending.

In my book, *Mind Your Hair*, I talk about makeover recipients (i.e., victims) who came to me literally crying for help. As much as my heart went out to them, there was only so much I could do.

A change in someone's appearance affects all parts of their life. Those made-for-TV makeovers were done by stylists who knew absolutely NOTHING about the people they worked on. They knew nothing about their needs, their goals, their tastes, their everyday life, and most importantly, their expectations. I desperately wanted to knock some real life awareness into those stylists and their ratings-obsessed producers.

That is when M first called.

When M introduced herself, I immediately recognized who she was—the owner of a successful brand. Her name was definitely a household word.

"How can I help?" I asked in my coolest, most professional voice.

"You were recommended as the go-to person for radical hair changes," she said, "and I desperately need a new everything in my life."

This was followed by a rambling list of all the things in her life she did not like, her hair, of course, being at the top of it. Hair is where we feel in control, a part we can dominate when all else goes wrong. Of course, she wanted an appointment ASAP and would pay whatever was needed—airfare, lodging, travel time, expenses—to make it happen.

As she carried on, I tried to understand the meaning behind her words. What was the reason for this urgency? What in her was crying out for help and looking to me for a quick fix?

"In preparing for an initial appointment," I told her, "especially when there will be drastic changes, I ask clients to collect images—put together a mood board—of the look they have in mind." M responded that she had done enough branding and marketing to know exactly what a mood board was.

I asked her to briefly state in writing why she wanted to change her appearance and what she hoped it would accomplish. I felt proud of myself for having asked her to move out of her comfort zone and face her fears. This was a milestone, not just for M but for me as well. There was a time when my shyness would have prevented me pushing someone in her position out of her comfort zone.

Two days later, I met M in a penthouse suite in a five-star hotel on Chicago's Michigan Avenue. When she greeted me, her hair was in a bun high up on her head. I could see already there had been months of neglect. The texture was dull and brittle. I also wondered why she had placed the bun so high. She was certainly tall enough. Why would she want to add inches to her height?

Immediately, M started to apologize for not having done her assignment. "I've been terribly busy . . . new product launch . . . so much to do . . ." while she led me to the absolutely gorgeous master bathroom. The red onyx fixtures and recessed lighting gave the whole room a glowy, dreamlike quality. This is where I was to set up my makeshift station

As she began to take down her hair, I saw it was even worse than I thought. Her hair had been colored so badly by many different stylists that there was a clear line of demarcation for each visit. Oy, then there were her straw-like neglected extensions. Although I thought I concealed my reaction at the time, she must have sensed what I was thinking.

M said, "I travel a lot so it's done by a lot of people... all with different ideas."

True, her hair had been bleached out and the style had no real direction and there was an overall lack of luster—not just in her hair—but in her life.

From the texture of her strands, I suspected malnourishment, a vitamin deficiency, probably folic acid and B12. I noticed that the bathroom countertops were literally covered with thousands of dollars worth of skincare products, yet her nails were brittle and her face was broken out.

I asked the obvious question: "Is there anything going on in your world right now, a life-changing event or major shift?"

"There's always something going on. That's my life... always something."

There was a bag of potato chips on the counter beside

her, the additive-filled, greasy kind. M didn't fully answer my question. Instead, she filled-up her mouth with potato chips. I knew I had hit a nerve.

While she was busy munching and swallowing, I looked more closely at her features. M had a graceful physical form, a long, graceful neck, high cheekbones, an elegant line like a ballerina. She is very beautiful, I thought. In my mind, I was already creating a new look for her.

She finished the chips and started twisting the empty bag into a ball. Then she extended this motion to her hair, nervously twisting and un-twisting a strand.

I took this to be a signal.

Ever so gently, I placed my hand over hers and held it there until the twisting stopped. Her eyes glistened and I saw they were hazel and almond-shaped, like a Persian cat.

Finally, she broke the silence. "There's a meeting coming up... it's important... I have to look good... my appearance will matter." Although I was curious about the meeting, I decided to focus on the job at hand.

"I understand," I said, "you didn't have time for the assignment, but there's time now." I scanned the room and saw a few magazines among the bottles and jars. "Show me pictures of how you think you'd like to look." She responded by rolling her eyes and wearily nodding her head.

"The pictures are for you as much as for me," I said. I remembered all the pictures I looked at before deciding on my Prince of Wales suit. "A new look can be a shock to your system. It's important for you to visualize it first."

However, she had her own way of thinking:

"I brought you here for your expert opinion. You're supposed to have an excellent eye." Then, as if daring or challenging me, she said, "You're supposed to be a genius. You're supposed to be Michelangelo."

Her words also struck a nerve. I was very young then and easily flattered. I knew she wanted a magic fix for the thing she didn't want to talk about. I also knew she was putting the fate of her appearance into the hands of a stranger.

They weren't just any hands, they were my hands. I had more than a little hubris, and my mind had already formed a clear image of how I wanted M to look.

So, I gave her my expert opinion.

I explained she would have a new kind of beauty, "it won't be the same as your old beauty." I wasn't sure if I was trying to warn her, reassure her, or both. "Time to let go of your extensions," I continued. "You don't take care of them, they're all wrong for your hair type, and they're just all wrong for you.

"Now for the color... while it's growing out, let's cover

the washed-out blonde with a warm, chocolate—it will be like your original color. Then I will paint splashes of light in just the perfect honey tone."

I can become very animated when I talk about something I'm passionate about. I was talking about painting and colors, and how I can apply tiny dabs so the mixing is done in the eye of the beholder creating a beautiful shimmer. (I'd spent many happy hours at le Musee' d'Orsay, Paris's temple to impressionist art.)

M, meanwhile, was beside herself with anticipation. She actually bounced up and down and made little girl noises. An observer watching us would have seen quite a spectacle. A voyeur in this massive suite in a luxury hotel bathroom big enough to be living space for a family of four, would see M squealing and clapping with a Frenchman gesticulating wildly with his hands.

Then they would see me go into my zone and make the magic happen.

When I create, I see nothing else. I've been told I look like a mad scientist, which is not surprising—I was trained by the great Mme. She taught us a special way to use scissors (it's not the normal way), and my scissors are always very large—Mme was big on *grand ciseaux*. I have mine made for me in Japan from the same steel they use for Samurai swords. My scissors are extensions of my limbs.

Five hours later . . . a masterpiece! I watched as M's entire being lit up. M had not seen her long, graceful neck and elegant bones for years.

"Oh my God, I'm a new person!" she exclaimed.

Now, this is what gets me every time—feeling I've made a difference. I left M's Michigan Avenue hotel suite that evening with a deep sense of satisfaction. I felt I'd done something worthwhile.

Then the following morning at 6:00 AM, just as I got off the plane in another city, I saw this message from M: "Call me ASAP. We need to talk."

A message like this is never a good sign. I took a deep breath, gathered my thoughts, and called.

On the phone, M's words were like a deluge. I retained only these three: "I hate it!"

Talking a mile a minute, M tried as best she could to explain how naked she felt without her old extensions. This feeling I understood. I had taken enough extensions off models after photoshoots to know her reaction was somewhat normal.

Then she said something that stunned me. In trying to tell me her hair was too dark, she used the word "black." When she first said it, I thought I didn't hear right. She kept repeating the word—black, black, black.

I wanted to say, "Dear lady, you are hardly naked and

your hair is not black, it's a beautiful, warm brown with honey-colored highlights."

Hair is so tied up with people's emotions, I decided not to argue facts with her. M was unhappy in her own skin. Yesterday's change was a temporary patch. When she faced her life again in the morning, her new look just did not fit her mindset.

Finally, when M exhausted herself venting I asked her, "What do you want?"

She wanted another appointment, same arrangement as before.

When we met again three days later—this time in Rio de Janiero—M's hair was hidden under a Gucci silk scarf. I tried not to take it personally.

I got right to the point: "You said you needed to look a certain way for an upcoming meeting. Who will be at that meeting? What is your purpose?"

She started to say, "My husband," then she said, "My ex-husband," and then, "My ex-to-be."

I had already guessed as much.

I believed—and still believe—we hold a lot of pain in our hair. I had naively hoped I could make M's life better by cutting the pain away.

I went back to the bathroom in my mind. When M took her hair down the other day, I saw it had distinct layers.

The blonde kept getting blonder and blonder while the extensions got longer and thicker. This wasn't the first time layers of hair told me the story of a relationship.

"We need to come up with a plan," I told her, "to satisfy your wish to retain elements of what you had, but also make it better." She seemed to like what I was saying.

"For it to be the right plan," I continued, "we need to be clear that there's a story going on behind what you hope to accomplish. When did you start wearing those extensions?"

She became very still and whispered, "In memory of a great week in Mykonos."

She told me about the girls on the beach, girls with long, flowy hair. Her husband had admired them and remarked about their hair reflecting sun and water and asked why M kept cutting her hair in a bob.

M told him she enjoyed her hair at shoulder length and liked how it played up her jawline and cheekbones. When her husband tapped into her insecurity she immediately ran off to a salon in London for her first set of extensions.

At first, her husband seemed happy with them. The extensions, after all, were to please him. He was getting his way. As expected, in time he started complaining. He blamed the extensions for getting in the way of their intimate moments.

So what did M do? She went back and added more extensions.

"I guess I was trying to get his attention and get back at him at the same time. He loved me as I was when we first met. He told me he loved my silky, brown hair. Then he started staring at blonde girls. 'California blondes are hot,' is how he put it. So I went blonde."

At that moment she brought up her ex-to-be's personal assistant. "Personal assistant... yeah, right! Scandinavian, half my age, five-foot-eleven, sure took her job to heart! Went waaaay beyond her job description."

I didn't have to ask M if the "assistant" had long blonde hair.

The bathroom in the Rio suite was done in white marble. One of the walls was covered with mirrors. I asked M to take off her scarf.

In that first moment of seeing her new look again—before she could think and let her baggage take over—M seemed pleasantly surprised.

"It might not be all that bad . . . my hair feels so silky now...I have good bone structure ...I used to always keep it short..."

"You liked the idea of bringing back your own hair and color when I suggested it," I said.

M said, "I thought it would make me the person I once

was. I wanted to start paying more attention to what makes me happy instead of twisting myself every which way . . . and for what? A cheating husband!"

"Then why, the next morning, did you ask me to come back again?"

"I was imagining I could seduce him one last time . . . how stupid! He has already moved in with his new girlfriend and has zero interest in me. I could be bald or cut off arm or have three facelifts—what I look like doesn't matter!"

"So now you are free to be your own person." I said this fully expecting M to tell me she changed her mind and really loves her new look. M didn't make things so easy. I watched as she spent a good few minutes staring into the mirror. Staring and scowling and becoming less attractive. Finally, she spoke:

"I liked the idea of my own hair and color because the blonde and the extensions were for him. Now when I look, I don't like what I see."

OK, I was prepared for this. I had brought along temporary extensions, the kind you clip on and take off. I could style them to blend with M's hair, give her a lesson in extension care and maintenance, and then have her practice putting them on and removing them.

As for the color, we kept the idea of M's own color by

keeping the dark base (so technically she would not be "blonde") and I would add even more and even lighter highlights—in M's words, a "happy halo of sunshine."

Six hours later, a miracle had been accomplished. M had had just enough change to feel "new," but not so much as to make her uncomfortable.

When I left, I felt relieved, just not satisfied. I never saw M after that. I sometimes think of her and wish her well. I know from my experience that mirrors reflect more than just our physical bodies. I just wish I had been able to convey that to M.

M's story is everyone's story at some point or another, including my own. Think back, when was the last time you made a radical change as a quick fix on the spur of the moment—making a big change without spending time to analyze the process? What happened next? Were you happy? Were you disappointed? Did you realize there is no "quick fix" in life? Did you take the time to discover what desire for change was really about? Can you see that in yourself or, like M, do you need an objective person to help?

CHAPTER 4

The Fashion Language

"*FASHION* IS WHAT YOU BUY – *Style* is what you do with it!"

"I wonder what it's like," the Frenchmen said, "all those supermodels . . . and those famous people!"

"Well, someone's got to do it," I humorously responded.

The man speaking was the baby-faced chubby kid like the one with the bad haircut who used to sit on top of me in the playground as a child. The scene was a party in my hometown attended by my former bullies. I was the guest of honor and they were giving me the rock star treatment.

It seemed strange, surreal in fact . . . thinking back to

when I first set my sights on *la célébrité*. I wanted to make my bullies jealous.

"I'm proud of you," one of them said. Another said, "So, now you're a jet-setter." As I listened to their embarrassed apologies, it seemed I was hearing them in a dream.

Later that night, in the house I grew up in, I went over what had happened. "If it weren't for my bullies," I thought, "I wouldn't be where I am now." I almost wanted to thank them. With that thought, something in me changed. I had had my sweet revenge. I was ready to move on.

When I returned to Miami, I felt unusually restless. In the weeks and months following, the feeling grew. My restlessness turned into frustration, and then a sense of being "boxed in."

I was still feeling that way while on a TV sound stage, where the CEO of a global men's clothing line was preparing for a televised apology. One of his employees had said something he should not have said and the CEO needed to undo the damage. I was there to style his hair.

When my client arrived in the changing area, he was wearing a black suit, a buttoned-up black shirt, a tie, and dark glasses. Immediately, the in-house stylist showed him a rack filled with men's clothing. My client just shrugged her off.

"I built a brand, I'm a fashion executive, and I'm very proud of my signature look."

I, meanwhile, tried to hold my tongue. I was his hairstylist, his *coiffeur,* which meant I was confined to the "hairstyling" box. Something inside me was screaming to get out. Then, something totally visceral happened. I let out a deep, guttural sound, and muttered to myself in French.

My client stopped in his tracks. "Is there something wrong with my outfit?" he asked with uncharacteristic vulnerability.

"You are talking to the press! You are here to *apologize*! Wearing that shirt and that outfit, believe me, the media will crucify you!"

He peered at me from over his dark glasses.

"You look like you are going to beat up someone," I said. I told him he needed to look "sympathetic and approachable." I actually reached out and took his glasses off him. That is when I saw the fear in his eyes.

I was able to convince him to change his shirt and found one in a friendly, honest-looking blue. I also convinced him to wear it without the tie, with the top button open. He drew the line, though, at changing his black suit. I used a Hermès pocket square of subtly patterned silk to offset its starkness of the black. It was blue and purple and I didn't fold it the way most people do. I accordion-ed it so it would fan out softly—just the right tiny touch to suggest spontaneity and softness.

A few weeks later, the same CEO asked me to sit in on a meeting with his buyers and marketers. He could not be there, but he sent instructions: "Please be sure my hairstylist Patrice is part of the conversation."

Hairstylist? The buyers were very skeptical of me. This meeting was about *clothing,* not hair, the stuff people wear from the neck down. However, the boss had ordered it so they had to include me. Their resistance was palpable. This was their turf and, in their minds, outside my "hair" territory.

After the introduction, I did what I do best when walking into a new territory—I observe! It allows me to understand the environment, their reaction, their body language, posture, voice pitch. At first, no one was truly interested in my opinion. Eventually my client kept returning to me to ask my opinion. Eventually, one person in the group shifted the energy by respecting my input and then seeking it out. By the end of the day I was a crucial part of the conversation. Eventually, I became part of every marketing and branding conversation for months on end.

Why do I tell you this story? We all have a tendency to "drink our own Kool-aid," buy the marketing strategy, not buck the system. This story shows you how by adding an expert on your team who can represent what the consumer "sees" is invaluable. It allows the team to look at things from a fresh perspective. It gives new meaning to an old idea. It shifts the *image* and maximizes the *impact*.

Where are you listening to your old story? Where do you need fresh "eyes"? Where can you add an expert from another field and maximize your *impact*?

* * *

Not long afterward, I once again felt that restless feeling of knowing I was more than the "super stylist." This time it was in Beverly Hills (I was by then a bi-coastal commuter). Late one afternoon, my client K walked into the salon. Actually, she lumbered in. Something had gone wrong for her that day. She seemed to be carrying the weight of the world.

K was in the entertainment industry. She made things happen behind the scenes. She was a powerhouse who out-swam the sharks. Needless to say, the sharks were all men. In contrast to this—and very likely *because* of it—she always wore a skirt. Never pants, not even a pants suit. Always *haute couture*. She didn't ask anyone for fashion advice. She thought she had it handled.

At that time, many businesswomen still made fashion decisions in order to fit into a man's world. K dared to be different. K dressed to stand out as a woman—a glass-ceiling smasher who got to where she was by being better than the men. Her clothes let you know it. They were form-fitting (why not?), *haute couture* (she could afford it), and on that particular day, she wore a to-die-for Karl Lagerfeld outfit that was pristine white. I believe she was sticking it to the boys in the boardroom—or anywhere else for that matter.

K was one of my salon regulars—people you would think would want house call appointments but opted for the salon instead. The regulars came to the salon to network and gossip—they all seemed to know one another—and let down their hair in more ways than one. Usually when K arrived, she would hang out for a while first. If you wanted to catch up with K, book an overlapping appointment.

Except on this day, K came in and collapsed without talking to anyone. She did not even bother to put on a robe or remove her pristine spotless white jacket, which was a fashion *objet d'art*. I actually had to hand her a robe and invite her to make herself comfortable, as my instinct wanted to protect this magnificent outfit. Then, after she had unwound for a bit, K blurted out this question:

"Do you think I'm overdressed?"

"Of course you're not!" a voice answered from a nearby chair. The voice belonged to K's BFF.

"You always look totally marvelous," the BFF continued. "And anyone who says otherwise is either jealous or doesn't know what they're talking about. What makes you think you are overdressed?"

K said "I met with my team today. They think I'm a bitch."

"What? No! Of course you're not a bitch. Did someone say that to your face?" asked the BFF.

"Not exactly, . . . but I sensed it," K replied.

K paused and thought for a moment. "I don't micromanage, I don't berate, I respect and value creative people. Even with all that, as I was leaving today, someone did say, 'Why are you getting your hair done now? It looks perfectly fine to me!'"

As K and her BFF were speaking, I was busy mixing K's colors. A buzzer sounded. The BFF's hair was ready. I would check on it, then have my assistant wash it.

I was already parting K's hair and applying color in tiny strokes when, in my mind, I started looking more closely at K's white suit. It was breathtaking! Literally! I actually gasped when she first walked in.

Lagerfeld had kept the Chanel refinements—classic details from the diva herself. That suit also made a startling statement. Blindingly white, perfectly cut and perfectly fitted—it demanded attention. You definitely owned the room when you wore it.

If you looked a little deeper, there was also another message in the suit's wool fabric. Your eye could not miss how *expensive* it looked. It is very hard for wool to be so very white. The wool has to be of sublime quality and only the most expensive designers can have it.

Now, glamour industries are notorious for getting people to work for low pay. Only the people at the very top get top dollar. Others work for love. I tried to imagine K, decked out in her in-your-face power suit, in a gritty roll-up-your-sleeves setting trying to lead and inspire a team of underpaid creative "others." K's suit was a fashion *faux pas* of the first order.

Despite the BFF's reassurances, K was emotionally falling apart. I was standing there next to her. I had my hands in her hair. I could feel her pain. No one would believe this was the K who projected a larger-than-life presence in every other setting. I decided she needed to hear what the BFF could not see and would not tell her.

"When I was in Paris," I began, "I wore a special designer suit. My suit told the world who I was and it was also my security blanket. Then I moved to southern Florida where nobody wore that kind of suit. I was out of place, yet I still needed to feel I was special, and the suit helped me feel that way. So I learned to dress down with elegance. AND I actually enjoyed re-inventing my style."

As I said this, I became aware of K scanning my outfit. She took in my custom shirt with its custom buttons and collar and cuffs lined in matching paisley fabric. Then she took in my dark-wash denims. My jeans were beautifully tailored, up the highest Saville Row standards. Even so, K recoiled when she saw them. Clearly, *jeans* were outside her comfort zone.

"I think I know where this is going," she said, cutting me off. "We call those things 'dungarees' where I'm from, and 'dungarees' are for cleaning the house."

By the time she finished telling me this, my mind had already formed a clear image of K in a dress-down outfit. I visualized her wearing very good jeans, a good silk blouse, gold earrings and chains, and shoes that cost a fortune. I wanted to tell her what I had envisioned, but after her remark, I decided this was not the right time. I tried another approach.

"White," I told her, "can mean purity, or it can make you look like a goddess. Because white also gets dirty, wearing it can mean you are above doing the "dirty" work you ask of your staff. They think anyone who does any "real" work can't possibly wear white all day and still look immaculate."

"What are you suggesting?" she asked.

"You can still have your gorgeous Chanel look, in one

of her famous nubby tweeds, and in a color more gentle to the eye."

K, I could tell, was listening. In fact, she was nodding her head in agreement—until the BFF chimed in again. Back from the shampoo area, her hair in a towel, the BFF wanted to get a few more words in before I started her blowout.

"Did I tell you," the BFF asked, "about that horrible date I was on? The guy had the friggin' nerve to say to me, 'Are you some sort of feminist control freak?' Shocked, I asked why, and the creep answered, 'You're all dolled up and I know it's to impress me. Are you trying to control the evening?'"

"What a rude and insecure idiot!" responded K.

"Exactly. If someone can't handle what you're wearing, I say 'the hell with 'em!' How can you expect to be a leader if you don't come in with winning energy?"

Given what had happened between my parents, I too was a crusader. I believed—and still believe—it's every woman's (and man's) right to wear whatever they damn well please. However, I'm also a pragmatist.

There was so much I wanted to say just then. I wished I had a podium. If only I could put into words all the things I thought, I knew, and I believed! Since it was time to dry the BFF's hair, and then it would be time to dry K's hair, I decided to wait. Whatever I might have said, whatever message was in me, was about to be drowned out.

I had not seen K or the BFF for few months when K unexpectedly texted me.

"Thank you, thank you, thank you for your help. Things have really turned around. The team and I are getting along fabulously. We have great creative synergy and I am having the time of my life! Take a look at my selfie."

"Wow!" I thought. "So, she must have gone for the nubby tweed after all!"

I could not wait for her picture to download. K's *faux pas* notwithstanding, I felt we were kindred spirits. I wanted to see how my fellow fashionista handled "true to oneself" while also being appropriate.

Then I saw the answer.

First I saw K's team—all smiles, funky t-shirts, a fun group. Then I saw K with the biggest smile of all.

K wore a white blouse, gold chains and earrings, big-ticket shoes, and—drumroll please—jeans!

K's outfit exactly matched the image I had in my mind! How could that be? My thoughts went to 100th monkey theories and telepathy programs where mental images magically travel from one person to another. Then it came to me: *Great minds think alike!*

Whether you are a type A personality or not, we all have

preconceived notions of what we think is fashionable or what looks good on us. What we do not know is if we are right. It is not until this very stubborn reasoning has costs you a date, a job, or a promotion. Has anyone ever said something to you about the way you dress that initially shocked you? After giving it some thoughts (without admitting it to the person's advice, of course!!!) did you apply the advice? Did it actually turn the situation around completely?

Do you need to know what your BFF will not tell you?

CHAPTER 5

Comfort Zones

OUR CLOTHES BECOME PART OF WHO WE ARE and sometimes it hurts to change them.

In New York, my long-time client D was about to undergo a big change. D was used to being in charge—of her time, her business, the people in it, everything—with one exception: her love life. A commanding presence in the boardroom, romantically, D was a slouch.

I learned this one Saturday, first thing in the morning, when she called saying she needed to see me . . . urgently. For D, this last-minute urgency was unusual, to say the least.

Turns out she had been invited to a dinner party that evening, where she was to meet a certain captain of industry—a "gentleman of interest." Now for D, a "gentleman of interest" had to be high enough up the food chain to not be intimidated by her position. That left slim pickings. Within that limited pool of eligible bachelors, D already had struck out with several of them.

"I need your help," D said. "I need help deciding what to wear." Knowing D as I did, I realized this was a big leap of faith for her. Her timing was perfect. I had just taken my own leap of faith. I added the proverbial "slash" to my professional description—I was now known as a "hairstylist/style and image coach."

An hour after D's call, I was ushered into D's Manhattan penthouse. It was flawlessly decorated with modern furnishings and art and collectibles from her many travels. D directed me to one of the side chairs surrounding a long glass table. D sat directly across from me. Her hair, as usual, was flat-ironed and pulled back. With D, everything was about control.

From across the table, D tried to tell me why the impending dinner meant so much to her. D was at a loss for words. She struggled to make sense of her many memories of disappointments and failure. Her personal life just was not working and she was desperate to know why.

"It always happens, every time without fail... the man's insecurity kicks in."

As D spoke, I zeroed in on how she was holding her body. She held herself upright, straight as an arrow. I noticed how she sat, how she crossed her legs. Her whole manner was about control. Someone watching her and not hearing her words might think this was a job interview and not a heart to heart discussion.

I could see how, in D's presence, the intimidation process happens. There is a little boy inside every man, whether he is a successful CEO or a stay at home dad. What do little boys want? To have fun and not be controlled by "Mommy."

Today—the clock was ticking...

I have worked under the gun before. Once on a Lear jet at 30,000 feet. Somehow that, by comparison, was a simple job. D felt she needed to project certainty by opting for a sleek updo with NO part.

I, however, would do just the opposite— a head full of flirty curls. Hair handled, what to do with the rest of her?

D needed to handle herself differently. She needed to project more fun and openness. The word "flow" came to my mind. Then I had a crazy thought: "D needs a body-language makeover."

Except body language is not something you can just flip

a switch to change. Actors can do it using memories and images, but D was never trained as an actor. I have learned to say "no" to clients who expect me to be a magician. I was starting to seriously wonder: Was I trying to do the impossible?

I will tell you now, I did find a fix for every one of D's body-language "shortcomings"—and it had nothing to do with magic.

The idea came to me in a flash while I was taking stock of D's wardrobe. I knew from personal experience how clothes can have a dramatic effect on the person wearing them. When D gave me the grand tour of her vast walk-in closet, I was already following a hunch.

It struck me that her entire wardrobe was built on three colors: grey, navy, and black. Every single garment she owned fit exactly the same way—tight as a glove (she worked out with a trainer daily). While D owned a closet full of garments and every day she changed her garment, did she ever really change her clothes?

D needed a new clothing experience. Her body and entire being needed new information.

I have learned over the years to respect my clients' comfort zones. As much as I would like to, I can't push someone to where they don't want to go . . . unless I know them very well and I know they need a little push. D needed that push.

"We're going shopping," I told her. "Your clothes have a job to do and there's nothing in your closet up to it."

Now D was an admitted label snob, so it was a given we would stick to luxury brands. That was just one of the criteria. Already I was thinking: *lightness . . . movement . . . joie de vivre . . . florals . . .*

Out and about in New York on a Saturday afternoon, I knew just what to look for. First on the list, Fred Joaillier, jeweler to the caviar crowd, for D's perfect earrings. We chose a pair of long chandeliers—the kind that dance when you move your head to create a sense of freedom and aliveness.

Then came the shoes with red-lacquer soles and heels as high as D could handle, which was quite high—D had core muscles. The pair we chose had low-cut vamps (also known as "toe cleavage") and were nude patent.

Next, Herrera for the dress itself . . . a floral fantasy in pastel organza. The bodice had a princess cut—again, the inverted pyramid and the skirt was actually flair! D had nothing flair in her closet.

Then, back to the penthouse for a remake of D's dead-straight, dark-brown ponytail. Again, the idea was to create "flow." Balayage highlights for depth and dimension . . . then, with my curling barrel, I created this gorgeous cascade of spirals, reminding us hair is alive and organic.

Finally, it was time to put on the new dress. D slipped into it and I helped with the zipper. Then she put on her shoes. Up on her toes, giggling and whirling, pretending she was a ballerina, D looked gorgeous! Everything about her seemed different.

"I'm finding my inner Cinderella," she said. The "new" D was ready for the evening.

The following morning, I waited impatiently. It was a quiet, overcast, New York Sunday morning. At just before noon, D texted:

"Lots to tell... how about brunch?"

Brunch was at a cafe across from Lincoln Center. When I first spotted D walking toward me from about fifty feet away, I nearly fell over. She glowed with femme power!

Then, over croissants and espresso, D shared her amazing evening—a symphony of compliments and positive feedback from all who were there, including one of her big investors.

And... what about the "gentleman of interest"?

D saved that part for last. Smiling to herself, a knowing smile that made me think of the Mona Lisa, D said, "We shall see."

Then she added, "Veeeeeery interesting..."

* * *

Not all of my clients are wealthy superstars, but they still need the same care and attention. Let's talk about B.

B came to me while I was still buzzing about the success of D, and B desperately needed HELP. Her wardrobe was the primary thing holding her back from the amazing future she was creating. It was built from remnants of her prior life as a competitive body builder where you dress so the judges can "see" all you muscles. She dressed to play to the judges' eyeballs.

She built her first successful business after body building on the phone from her home office where her old wardrobe was perfectly adequate. Her new venture, however, would require in-person meetings and public appearances. This posed a huge problem!

The first time I saw her was at a speakers' event. I actually did a double take—and not in a good way. Remember Julia Roberts in *Pretty Woman* BEFORE she had her new wardrobe? That is what B, ex-body builder, looked like, except even more glitzed up. With the rest of the group in business casual, I wondered what was she thinking?

Of course, she knew her clothes were a problem. She did, after all, hire me—and was a battle. Still, she was super determined and she knew her future depended on dressing appropriately for her new role.

B was addicted to popping eyeballs. There are many different kinds of attention, and each gives us different energy. B was used to one kind. She needed to learn how to experience another to succeed in her new business.

Off we went to a discount outlet where we picked up twenty-five pieces all coordinated to go with one another, complete ensembles, with variations. Shopping turned out to be the *easy* part. When we got back and she saw the new items laid out on the bed, B went into a tizzy.

She was completely confused about what to wear when and with what. As I proceeded to begin the list of what, when and how to coordinate outfits, B got distracted. She went to her dressing area and came back wearing . . . well, you can imagine. Then she asked me what I thought of it. AND I TOLD HER. AND SHE LISTENED.

When I started working with B, there were women who refused to be in the same room with her. These same women now give her standing ovations. As for B's new way of dressing, it is part of her new personal brand.

D and B are both part of something universal: we become attached to our clothes. We become attached to how we think we look in them. We become attached to how we feel in them. We become attached to how people react to us in them.

I believe in goal-oriented dressing—getting your appearance to align with what you are trying to accomplish. D and B certainly had goals—very different types of goals. The similarity between them is that they were both emotionally ready. They were at a breakpoint and open to change and willing to get coaching to achieve their goals.

We all are guilty of an emotional attachment in clothing, appearance, or else, which becomes a habit, good or bad, until we finally break free from it. After reading about D and B, do you see yourself a little in either of them?

Are you finally ready to embrace a change and beak free from the emotional bond of your wardrobe? Are you ready to realize how much empowerment you can have? Are you ready to remove your garments and *change* your clothes?

CHAPTER 6

When Is a Shoe Not a Shoe?

When I hear someone say, "I won't be dictated to by fashion," I ask, "Who determines fashion?"

The answer is, of course, "We the People."

The fashion industry stays in business by giving us— "We the People"—what we want to wear.

The fashion industry follows trends like gender issues, the environment . . . whatever is going on.

The fashion industry stays in business by being part of the conversation.

It helps us say what is on our minds.

Not all that long ago, in San Diego, I spent three days in an over-air-conditioned hotel ballroom while my technophobic brain was being hammered by people to whom fashion was an F-word.

It was as if I had landed on a strange new planet. It was also a natural next step after what I am about to share.

When I was a boy, I was not athletic. My father hated me for it. I became even more un-athletic. Once an ocean came between us, something in me shifted. In Miami, I became a gym rat. For a trainer, I chose a macho man who actually reminded me of my father. Except my trainer sissy-shamed me because he wanted to help me. In return, I clothes-shamed him. I teased him about not tucking his shirts in. He teased me into getting ripped.

It was with my buff and proud new body that I returned to France to keep an old promise—to free my mother and siblings. I paid off the mortgage on the family home, then bought out my father's share. Mission accomplished! The old man vanished from our lives forever.

With this turning-point finally behind me, I experienced another shift. I always knew my fear of technology came to me courtesy of my father. Now I could also acknowledge his gift.

My father was a man of many talents, one of which was painting. He could look at a photograph and paint it from memory, and do so in any size with perfect linear perspective. Ever since my earliest years, I have had a near-photographic visual memory and could photo-edit mentally. Quite a wonderful gift from a man who did not want to give me anything!

The event in San Diego was an eCommerce bootcamp—a 3-day deep dive into the world of digital marketing, technology included. On the first day, I arrived early and positioned myself front-row-center (to keep from falling asleep). Then I walked around and people watched.

There were definitely no fashion plates among them. Hardly anybody's clothes really fit well (by my standards). I did see a scattering of business suits, but their wearers turned out to be presenters. One presenter started by telling us that the suit was his wife's idea and she bought it for him that very morning. The way it fit him made me think of an uncomfortable ten-year-old at a wedding.

As usual, I wore jeans. Now, there are many cuts and kinds of jeans and many ways to wear them. For this event, I left out the black blazer (another one of my go-to fashion statements). I also did not wear my couture-quality jeans. You know the ones I wear to make a statement with a tuxedo jacket.

For the seminar, I chose classic Levis with an impeccable fit. The great Steve Jobs always dominated the room from the moment he walked in—in his great fitting Levis. They too were just the right wash to go with his trademark black t-necks.

The program started with a keynote presentation. To my astonishment, there were parts I understood. Especially the part about branding. Branding was the buzzword of the day. Show me your uniqueness, tell me your story, and beam it to me instantaneously. In short, it was about visual communication, which was right up my alley.

In fact, I was so intent on what I was hearing, that I wasn't distracted by the people sitting near me. At least, not for a while. When someone or something is visually out of whack, I can't help but notice. There was a man sitting next to me who was most assuredly visually out of whack.

He was big, about six-four with massive shoulders and an industrial-sized beer gut. Yet somehow, he managed to find trousers too big even for him. They bunched into huge folds around his belly. He wore an old t-shirt that looked like he had slept in it, and his shoes were . . . ah, strange. They were dull black, the color of coal, made from some plastic material, and they flared out at the toes. They reminded me of those giant foot pads at the bottoms of lunar landing vehicles.

What was most disconcerting about this man was his hairstyle, or lack thereof. The man was losing his hair.

Whatever hair he had left was cropped close to his head with one notable exception—he had very full, unruly sideburns which he let grew long. This resulted in two tangled thickets jutting out from either side of his head. They looked like antennas. If only he'd had green skin, he would be a dead ringer for Shrek, the cartoon character.

There was a slender man sitting on his other side who was obviously with him. The two exchanged notes and spoke to each other in a foreign language. The slender man wore a suit—a very formal suit—yet he wasn't a presenter. The suit was faded and vintage 1990's, double-breasted, over-stuffed shoulders, wide trousers, pleated at the waist.

Being a gregarious human, I tend to bond with whomever is seated next to me. This included my *Shrek* look-alike neighbor. I wanted to peer under that balding scalp, buzz cut, and sideburns and find out what made him tick. I sat with my curiosity for three days.

Then late in the afternoon on the last day when the seminar I turned to S (for *Shrek*), introduced myself and asked how he enjoyed the seminar. He answered with a routine "very much," then gave me his card and his elevator pitch.

I learned he was a B2B software developer who specialized in something called "security solutions." Recently, he developed some new something—"No one else knows how to do it" —and the reason he came to the seminar was to find out how to re-invent his business.

Then it was my turn. I had neither card nor pitch. I came to the seminar because someone I knew had an extra ticket. I thought of telling him, "I'm a recovering technophobe and I'm here for immersion therapy." Instead I let him talk.

S told me he had once been wildly successful. When he first started out, he was the only one around. Then competitors moved in on him. The competitors, S told me, were by-the-book corporate types who did not have half his chops. "Why," he lamented, "should it be so hard for me to compete with my inferiors?"

He railed against his fate, the unfairness of the universe, his competitors, and the decision makers who, for some inexplicable reason, never showed him his due respect.

I asked, "When you talk to these decision makers, do you meet with them in person?"

"Of course! There is no other way. It must be one-on-one," said S.

"When you meet with them, what do you wear?" I asked.

"What? I wear clothes," S snapped, as if I had asked a stupid question.

Meanwhile, the man in the suit shot S an "I told you so" glance.

All the while my brain was still spinning from three days of information. I was thinking about the slides we saw of eye-tracking heat maps—technology for seeing how our eyes respond to on-screen information—when an idea started to crystallize in my mind.

"There's a language of appearances," I told S. "And if you want to be trusted and taken seriously, or even heard, you cannot rely on just words. You have to be visually literate. You can try to convince yourself appearances don't matter, but it's a lie. If you fall for it, you're finished."

S gave me a confused look, he had no idea what I was talking about. I tried again.

"Appearances," I said, "speak directly to our intuition. Our intuition sees things our thinking brains don't notice. Change a typeface, or the color of a logo, or the shape of a frame around a graphic, and it changes how people respond to your webpage."

Of course, I was not just talking about webpages. I was addressing S's blind spot. Predictably, he nodded, said, "Hmmm . . . very interesting," and changed the subject by introducing me to his suit-wearing buddy.

They were both from the same town in Norway. When I asked S's buddy what he learned from the seminar, S answered for both of them. S said they came to re-invent themselves and they learned too many things to start listing them now. Then S invited me to join them for a beer. Theirs was clearly a relationship where one was the leader and the other the go-along.

As we stretched our legs in the afternoon sunlight and S looked for a suitable beer bar, I planned my next move. I now knew I needed to tell these two gentlemen what I did and how I could help them.

The ale house was cozy, funky, low key. We found a quiet booth and a waiter took our order. Big, hulking S sat on one side by himself. He and I faced each other directly. It was my chance to talk.

Here's how I started . . .

"I know you came here and sat for three days because something in your life is not working. You took a lot of notes, you learned some new things, but you didn't learn the one thing you must do to turn your business around, maybe even your life. Do you believe things happen for a reason?

S stared at me, curiously.

"Of all the people in that enormous ballroom you sat next to me. And it just so happens, I'm the person who can help you." I said this with total conviction and authority.

S's eyes widened.

"Helping people with your problem is what I do for a living."

"What do you do? Tell me!" said S.

"I will," I answered, "but first I need you to bear with me." I paused, and then said, "Allow me to read your hair."

"What!!?"

"Allow me to read your hair."

"My what!!?

There are no words to describe the look on both men's faces. At first, S just pointed to his bald spot; he was too stunned to laugh. Then he and the other man looked at each other and both started to laugh like hyenas.

"A hair reading! On my bald head! How can anyone know anything about me from my bald scalp and buzz haircut?"

They were still laughing when our drinks arrived. I had to shield three overflowing beer mugs from their uproarious thigh slapping.

Finally, the laughing stopped. They raised their pints and waited for me to tell them the rest of the joke.

I was not joking. I had already done hair readings to entertain audiences and I was actually quite accurate. When you have seen as many scalps and crowning glories as I have and heard as many true confessions, well... your brain just puts two and two together.

I asked S again, "I am asking your permission. May I read your hair?"

"Are you some kind of fortune teller?"

"No, I am very scientific.

"Scientific? Oh, come on!"

"Yes. This is based on scientific research I started when I was nine."

I said this with a straight face and S was suddenly incredulous. For a nanosecond, he gazed at me wide eyed. Then he quickly rearranged his face into a patronizing smirk.

"Go ahead . . . Read my hair!" said S.

S was daring me. I dared him back, "Are you sure you can handle it? It can get personal."

S answered by crossing his arms. I knew what his posture meant. OK, I went for it.

"When a man loses his hair," I said, "he has to make a decision. Should I hide it? Do nothing? Or shave it all off, which is to say, 'So, I'm bald . . . deal with it!' You haven't made a decision. You are sitting on the fence, holding on for dear life to those last few wisps, torn between two ways of being. Am I right? I think you know I might be talking about more than just your hair. How am I doing?"

S shot me an "I'm on to you" grin and addressed his friend in English. The English was for my sake. "I think you are in on this," he said. "What did you tell him?"

"Nothing! How could I? We were always together."

S scratched his bald scalp. His theory had been shot down. Then I saw him fidget nervously with the gold band on his left ring finger.

I continued, "Whatever you do or don't do with your hair broadcasts a message. The same goes for your clothes. All the stuff you wear and put on tells others who you are, who you think you are, and more importantly, how they should respond to you. Shall I continue?

S raised both his arms in the stop motion used by traffic cops. "OK," he said, "you made your point. Why don't you read my friend here?"

I could see his friend was uncomfortable but did not want us to know it. I proceeded. He had a full head of hair and the cut was generic. His clothes, however, were interesting.

"From the way you look," I told him, "you were successful in the 1990's. Those were your glory years, the era of your highest professional achievements, perhaps in your personal life, too."

He nodded.

"Then you hit a downturn, a very long and drawn out downturn. You tried to believe your old life would come back again, but that was not to be."

He nodded again.

"You came to the seminar hoping for a change. I believe

you are finally ready. In these last three days, did you learn how you can re-invent yourself? Tell me, what is your take-away?

"Um . . . probably, I should start recording my sales talk on video."

When he said that, I knew it was my moment. That is when I revealed I'm a celebrity hairstylist turned style and image coach. My clients are prominent business leaders.

"I don't know anything about your business," I continued, "but I do know something about CEOs. If you're pitching to CEOs, you have to look the part. CEOs can be clothes snobs."

"I always wear a tie and a business suit."

"I hope not that suit. It will sabotage you every time. By wearing that suit you're still holding on to some dream of once-upon-a-time. Want to re-invent yourself? Start by changing your clothes.

I was about to give S's friend a lesson in goal-oriented dressing 101. Then S chimed in, "When you read my hair before, you didn't say anything about my clothes. Is there something I should know about what I'm wearing?

S's Viking warrior facade was starting to crumble. There was a child under that massive form.

"Do you want me to read your clothes?" I asked.

"Please."

I started by saying, "I already see from your clothes you don't trust yourself . . ."

What???

"Look at the way your trousers fit. You are a big guy, finding your size must be hard enough. Did you pay more to get three sizes bigger?"

"I paid a little more, that is true, but I might end up saving long term. What if I gain weight?"

"That's just what I mean! You don't trust yourself."

I paused to let my words sink in. Then I brought up his shirt. "How long have you had it?"

S hesitated, he had to think. I saw he had that far-off look people get when they are trying to remember something. Finally, he spoke.

"I am not a good looking guy so I never paid attention to my appearance. Now you are this fancy French fashionista and you walk right into people's heads. I am leaving later tomorrow and I want to have something to take back with me. What is one thing I can buy here now?"

That was a question I didn't have to think about. I told S, "You need new shoes."

"Shoes? What is wrong with my shoes? They are black, nobody sees them."

"If I walked in here in a black tuxedo, what would you see?"

"I would see you are elegant and very fancy."

"I wouldn't be invisible, would I?

He thought for a moment, then shook his head "no."

"Your shoes are not invisible either," I continued. "Give me your number and I'll text you instructions, there's a store you can go to tomorrow. I'll send a picture of what you should buy. They will be the tuxedo of shoes but you will be able to wear them with anything. They'll make whatever else you're wearing look a thousand times better."

We spent several minutes fumbling with our phones. I found a picture as well as store directions, which I sent to S along with the words: *"Ferragamo, classic, signature buckle, black."*

Now, Ferragamo is an iconic brand made famous in Hollywood in the 1920's. In Italy, Florence to be precise, there is even a Ferragamo museum devoted to the brand's story. When you wear an iconic brand, you are not just wearing an article of clothing. You are wearing an image and have all the associations from that brand's legacy. I tried to explain this concept to S, knowing it was as foreign to him as the things he knew were to me. He seemed to catch on.

"So, these will be my power shoes. I will be at the store first thing when they open."

When I told S about Ferragamo, I purposely omitted a detail: *The price*. I wanted him to actually go there and experience high-end luxury shopping. I knew the level of C-suite executive S has to meet with. I wanted him to "walk in their shoes." I did not expect him to buy a pair.

The following morning, I waited in the hotel lobby where coffee was being served. S's friend was there wearing his old suit but no tie and he was carrying his jacket. S had already texted to say he had discovered a whole new world. He also said he had a heart attack when he saw what things cost.

Finally, S appeared. More accurately, he made a grand entrance. He literally moonwalked into the lobby and proceeded to do a victory dance. It was quite a spectacle. He was still the same big-oaf cartoon character as well as a Viking warrior. He was wearing the Ferragamos!

About six months passed after that. Then one day I heard from him. Since I had last seen him, S and his wife had separated, and he'd shaved off his sideburns.

Over Skype, S explained he had a new contract in the offing—the biggest job of his career. His proposal had been reviewed by corporate IT and now he needed to impress the CEO. It would be the most important meeting of his life. What should he wear?

S became my coaching client and we scheduled a series

of web meetings. I told him to window shop and look at pictures, and I gave him a list of what he would need. From the suit to the belt to the cufflinks and pocket square, we talked about his options for each and whether they aligned with what he needed to accomplish. His purpose.

Then S's big day came. When I heard from him afterwards, his first words took me by surprise. "Remember you once asked me what I thought about coincidences?" he said. I vaguely remembered saying something of the sort.

S then described being ushered into an impressive glass and steel office where he was greeted by the man himself—the man who would determine his future. First thing, the CEO looked down at S's shoes. Then he pointed to his own shoes, they were just like S's but in a different color. Then he told S he had a black pair at home and he owned them in every color.

"For the whole meeting," S said, "it was all he talked about. He liked my shoes, he liked me, and I got the contract!"

There it was. A man's future and the security of a corporation hinged on a tiny detail. I remembered when, at age eleven, I urged my mother to change something she wore.

Our lives are made up of unexpected outcomes of

chains of events set off by details. Sometimes these details are things people wear. I am honored to have been a catalyst for S to go from the brink of bankruptcy to a multimillion dollar deal with a pair of shoes.

* * *

Have you ever thought that you can change ONLY ONE thing about your appearance and your whole world will turn around? What is your ONE thing? What would you dare wear or change to completely transform your message?

Your image tells your life story to the world. How do you tell yours? By ONLY changing ONE thing, you can change the story of who you are when walking into a room?

CHAPTER 7

Hair Does the Talking

THE MOST IMPORTANT KEY TO SUCCESS—next to talent, of course—is an individual style.

There used to be a great divide between celebrities and the rest of us. Celebrities were the people we saw on the screen; the rest of us were the people who watched them.

Then the world changed.

Before it did, when the screen was still an un-scalable mountain and the people on it were gods and goddesses, I remember the fluttering in my stomach, the white noise in my head, and the feeling I was walking on sacred ground as I entered the lobby of the historic Beverly

Wilshire (where they filmed *Pretty Woman*) early one Oscar Day morning.

I was a kid of twenty-one, and I was about to do the hair of two A-listers, including a nominee.

My work, my art, my *pièces de résistance* were about to be televised, written about, talked about, seen on celebrity heads all over the planet!

Being at the Oscars that first time was for me the realization of a secret dream. I had imagined it would be like winning the lottery, meeting the love of your life, Christmas and nirvana all rolled into one. When it happened, it was more like walking a tightrope with eggshells on it while staring into the abyss. In short, it was no la-la experience.

Yet, I returned to the Oscars the following year, and kept returning. My publicist (who also agented my bookings) kept upping the ante until I was juggling seven regulars, all of them screen luminaries.

Now, screen luminaries are hard-driving perfectionists. They have to be. When they are dressing to look freaking fantastic for their moment of impact on a zillion eyeballs...

Well, it wasn't uncommon for a luminary to, let's say, ask for a "romantic" look because they planned on wearing boho-chic. We would agree on long, poetic tresses, and I would begin balayaging their hair and matching the extensions, but then their producer or agent or someone would tell them (you wouldn't believe the politics behind red-carpet dressing), "Go with a techno-chic, minimalist look." Then I would have to rethink everything (same goes for the makeup and wardrobe stylists). Plus, we're always working under the specter of very real fashion police, those "Ten Best" and dreaded "Ten Worst" lists.

For all the buzz around red-carpet hairstyles, the stylist almost never gets credit. Of course, the stylist can and will be blamed if someone's look gets a thumbs down. (I learned to say "no" to celebs with certain requests to keep that very thing from happening.) When your client looks amazing—and I made sure mine did—unless you have a "special arrangement" (I didn't), you are literally a Hollywood secret. I had to sign away my bragging rights. To this day, I am forbidden from revealing whose hair I've done.

They say, "Be careful what you wish for!"

I believe things happen for a reason. When it came to pass and destiny placed me in that holy of holies, the Oscar green room, a new purpose took hold in my life.

I had put a lot of energy and ingenuity into overcoming my once crippling shyness. And in those nail-biting moments behind the scenes when I had to be the Rock of Gibraltar to people I had once idolized, I looked back over my life and realized I'd discovered a tool, a process, a way of thinking (which you already know if you've been doing the exercises), and it was just what my stars needed.

When the time came for me to move on—because I no longer needed famous names in order to feel important—I had honed my skill for sharing what my life experience had uniquely taught me.

Meanwhile, as I told you, the world had changed. Now screens were everywhere, and so were ways of getting on them.

Celebrity had become democratized.

One day, as I was scrolling through my social media feed, I felt that chalk screeching on a blackboard feeling. It was my old paleo instinct telling me something was out of whack. I looked closer.

The words "forward thinker" jumped out at me. Yet the man in the accompanying headshot looked anything but. His hair, which was center-parted, tucked behind his ears, all one length, and longish, had that 1990's college-kid look. "Why," I wondered, "would a 'forward thinker' wants to be seen looking so last century? Promoting the future and looking trapped in the past? Where is the alignment between his professional and personal message with his hair? What business owner would hire him when there is no consistency form credentials to visual?"

* * *

Lucas (his real name) had a likable face. In his profile, he described himself as "purpose-driven" and "interested in natural healing, positive thinking, and the power of mind." I also saw he was looking for work—work as a paid public speaker. Another thing about Lucas: If I had been a web-marketing guru, I would have told him he needed a USP (Unique Selling Proposition)—a unique story, attribute, or quality (aka, "personal branding") to set himself apart.

But I'm an appearance guru, so for now I just focused on Lucas' hair, the first obvious message to convey his personality, his Brand. I decided to be daring and send him a direct message. Unless I am invited to, I NEVER do this sort of "intervention." My intuition was stronger than usual and stepping back, I am so glad I did it!

Now, Lucas and I have different recollections of our initial communication. I recall very clearly starting the conversation by politely asking, "What kind of responses are you getting from your profile?" Lucas just remembers being told, "You have a handsome face, but your hair is lousy." It is all about perception. Perception is emotion. Emotion is Branding.

In either case, Lucas was curious and open to hearing more. We agreed to meet over the phone (he was not ready yet to do a face-to-face meeting) for a 15 minute consultation which ended up lasting... an hour! By demonstrating my Image Impact Index, I was able to show Lucas how he could improve his Brand instantly by changing one thing on himself...his hair! With this single transformation, his life turned around. Now his vision, mission, and purpose aligned perfectly with his presentation.

Turns out, he had for years worn his hair in a long ponytail. Then he decided to donate his hair to a charity for cancer patients. So he went to the donation center and had it cut off—just cut, no shaping, no styling—and his headshot was taken a few days afterward (not a smart move). So, of course, we met again over the phone so I could explain why and how a haircut is a crucial way to express his personality, his message, *his brand*.

"I was diagnosed with multiple sclerosis (MS). Now I lead many different wellness communities. My purpose and obligation in life is to help more people in the world become aware of their body's ability to naturally heal itself. While being diagnosed, I began thinking about how this new path was a positive thing. By focusing on improving different areas of my life each day, I know that my 'Life Sentence' is the best gift I ever received.

"Patrice's personal direct message initially came to me as a surprise but done so brilliantly he intrigued me to know more about myself and the way my picture could tell the world my story accurately and efficiently, without discounting my lack of fashion sense!

"It also made me realize the emotional attachment to my hair and the fear of letting go. Cutting my hair exactly the way Patrice directed with his mood board to keep on point with my Brand, I finally understood the empowerment it provided me (you want to talk about a rush of positive energy!!!) and the direct link between emotions and image. It was my very first a-ha moment!

Wow! Talk about having a unique story of quality! Talk about setting yourself apart! I wanted to cry when I read it! This was the perfect reminder for me to know why I have been working so hard to put this step-by-step process together and help the world! This was an incredible reward.

No matter how often I see it, I still wonder how many people are missing the mark of their brand based on their hair.

Life is an evolution in all areas of your life. When was the last time you changed your hairstyle? When was the last time you checked on how accurate your hair is telling your story? When was the last time you understood what you are conveying with your haircut and style?

CHAPTER 8

The Worst of Me Is the Best of Me?

BEAUTY IS ALL ABOUT ATTITUDE.

Actors often say their roles don't become real for them until they wear their characters' clothes. The same applies here. Unless your new role can be played in your birthday suit, you have some work to do.

The conquest for thin and thinner has always been part of the runway, magazine, and editorials, the seventies especially when women were considered looking great with very little chest, super narrow waist, and no butt at all. Diet companies made it their mission to blast how to be thinner and thinner.

Suddenly who appears in the late nineties? *Jennifer Lopez!*

From chasing the ultra thin model body type to, little by little, curvy and big booty started showing up here and there. Once considered fat or cheap. Then, of course, was turning point with THE dress.

J. LO wore an exotic green Versace silk chiffon dress to the 42nd Grammy Awards ceremony on February 23, 2000. The sheer fabric was printed with a tropical leaf and bamboo pattern, and cut with a very low neckline that extended well past Lopez's navel, while the waist of the dress was studded with citrines.

Since this very moment big butts became a cultural point of reference. Women will loan their new born in order to put implants, getting fat transfer or any other surgical means to enhance their derriere . . .

Small noses were always a *thing*. Society created this belief if the nose was thin and the tip was pointing up it was a sign of cuteness, essentially remembering childhood where this little mischievous facial feature to look "cute" to the point of becoming a trend. For many girls in America, they would receive this gift of surgery on their 16th birthday. Then, who shows up with the biggest nose you can find and made it such a statement it actually was and always been her trademark?

Barbra Streisand. Because of these very facial trade, her voice is unique because of the nostril airways, creating a specific way for the oxygen flow to go through, therefore made an international career from what once upon a time considered the most horrible thing you could have on your body.

Small chest was very much part of the model world, the smaller the better. In fact, if not at all was the best thing you could possess therefore hired on the runway, in commercials, or for ad campaigns.

Suddenly, in the 90s, TV shows started popping up like crazy. Then, who changed the whole mindset about small breasts? *Pamela Anderson*. While proudly owning her skimpy red bathing suit, her lead role in *Baywatch* went from women should be flat to women should have big boobs wearing them as the best fashion statement! She set the trend by harboring fake boobs, going from once considered trashy, or else a secret if you would do a surgery of that sort (you would never tell a soul not even your best friend) to shouting on the top of the roofs you had implants put in, therefore you became a real fashionista and much more, the object of desire for men!!!

Coco Chanel definitely was all about female and

empowerment and yet the more you hide the more feminine you are, therefore the classier and more elegant. Who, after a painful divorce pronounced on March 29th 1978, was there to change the rules of feminism and empowerment by showing skin?

Tina Turner. The dresses got shorter and shorter and her legs became the beacon of what a woman is all about! Defying the rules of age as well because society said the older you get the more you cover up. Well she made the world think again because legs and showing them all the way until XXX rate limit became a fashion statement of the present and the future.

Last but not least, how about the hair? While wearing a wig or putting all kind of fake addition to your hair was once considered horrible, fake, and really low class went to becoming the trend of trends. Who started back in the 80s, way before everyone, who could simply care less about other people's opinion to saying to the world if you have thin hair or bad hair or simply you want to make your hair a statement?

Cher of course! She was definitely the pioneer of showing you can go from long brunette with bangs to blue edgy hair from one day to the next and not worrying about people knowing you are wearing fake hair. Because of this very statement, it then escalated to the world of hair extension we know now, to the point of today's world, if you are not wearing extensions you are actually out of the loop when once considered so horrible and tasteless.

Richard Branson. Of course we recognize him for the scruff, his longish hair, sort of the Boho style of clothing. Great. What is vision, mission, and purpose? What do we know him for? For one, saving the planet and saving animal kind.

Oprah Winfrey known as Oprah. On a marketing and branding perspective? Genius. We don't even need her last name to know whom we are talking about!

We don't remember her from her hair, her clothing, her fashion style impression. What is Oprah's brand? She is knocking at people's doors, giving money, houses, and cars away, and perhaps going to Africa to build schools for kids. Amazing.

That's what I'm talking about now we go much further than just the envelope and the thing we see from the exterior it's really going deeper in the core of the person and it is called... *spirituality!!!*

Imagine if I said that to you earlier on? What would have been your reaction? Now you start getting it!!! There is so much more to your story than just clothes or your "best" feature.

What is your worst? Nose, eyes, body shape, hair, too

tall, too short, too rich, too poor? Learn from those above and embrace your difference. Make your pain point your statement point. I can help you see that the worst of you is actually the best of you!

CHAPTER 9

All About You

"Adornment, what a science!
Beauty, what a weapon! Modesty, what elegance!"
—Coco Chanel

LET'S GET IN THE CLOSET, JUST YOU AND I, with the famous Spring cleaning, the new resolution when a new year comes, or else a sudden desire to purge.

The concept seems easy: I will give away what I have not worn in 5 years, toss what does not fit me anymore, get rid of my outdated pieces. Seems so simple, right?

Think again.

If you have been procrastinating, there is a reason! When walking into your closet, it is not about the *clothes* but facing YOURSELF—your emotions, your past, your body weight, your fears, your memories yes... YOURSELF.

Let me share a story with you.

When helping my CEO client a few days ago, she decided to "Give herself a new start!" Well, not quite. As ready as she thought she was, when walking in this fairly large size closet, all I saw was an explosion of patterns, styles, and colors. Years after years of compulsive shopping, jackets not needed right now but will find its useful moment who knows when, dresses I did not know were made out of so little fabric, styles so out of style 1993 called my cell because they wanted their pieces back!

Methodically, I started with all the clothes that still had the tags on them. You know, that moment in time when you don't feel very good in life right now, you buy a little something to feel better about yourself. Yes, this piece, still in your closet with the tag on because the day after the purchase, your emotions being in a different place took over and you said out loud, "What was I thinking?" Does this ring a bell with you?

As I am pulling the "new" clothes out, her reaction was what I hear the all the time:

Client (C): No, please, I want to keep it for now, it was expensive.

Me (M): Why is it still here with the tag attached to it?

C: I never found the right occasion to wear it, but one day, I am sure!

M: Why did you buy it then? Tell me...

C: I am not sure...

M: Do you remember when you bought it?

C: Not exactly...

M: Another question, how did you feel that day, do you remember?

C: Yes, I believe so...

M: Do tell...

C: I was feeling down, overwhelmed with work, sort of lonely, so shopping therapy was the perfect fix.

M: What is *the* perfect fix? What reward is the perfect fix? How is the fix?

C: Well it made me feel better to buy this jacket!

M: This jacket you never wore, with the label and the price tag still on it?

C: I know...

M: How long did this feel good last? Honestly?

C: That evening.

M: When you came home, what did you do with it? Did you try it on again? Did you enjoy the purchase?

C: Actually, that part I do not remember so well, I think I went to my closet and hung it up.

M: That was it? It stayed in the garment bag ever since?

C: Yes, in fact I forgot about it.

M: Just to make sure I am following you, this incredible reward lasted the time of purchase, faded in the closet and died down until today?

C: Well, when you put it that way...

M: No, no please, tell me if I did not understand correctly!

C: (sigh, long sigh) I guess you are right.

M: This is not about being right, it is about comprehending your purchase and why this item is still here, brand new. Why do you think?

C: At the time it seemed like a great idea...

M: And now?

C: Not so much.

M: Why?

C: Because you make me realize it was a waste...

M: A waste?

C: Yes, because if it is still here intact, I did not need it then…

M: What should we do with it then?

C: Throw it away? Give it? Keep it? I don't know!

M: Before making a decision, let's look at all the other items with tags on…

C: No, no, no please!!!!!

M: Why?

C: Are you going to ask me the same question?

M: Yes, I will

C: So, NO, please

M: Why? You remember we are here for what you called your new start right yes? No?

C: Yes, but . . .

M: But?

C: I did not think it was going to be this painful.

M: Painful? It should be fun!

C: That's what I thought, but I just realized something…

M: Yes?

C: Everything I bought which still have the price on were bought with the same sort of mindset.

M: What mindset is that?

C: The one I see now. It was either loneliness, lack of something, not like depressed, but definitely not a good place.

M: All right, so let's move on then.

C: Yes, please (with tears in her eyes).

Looking around, I asked to see the dresses so we can go over each style and their purpose. Responding to my visual instinct, I see this Chinese red dress, lycra looking material and so . . . small!!! I turn around and I see her now blushing. As I pull the hanger out, I realize the length or else lack of. . . . So short I actually wondered if it was a tube top of some sort. So immediately I asked:

M: Can you tell me about this dress?

C: Well, I bought it for a date.

M: A date? A romantic date? A night on the town with the girls? A night at the club?

C: A date with this guy I met at the gym.

M: OK, so why this dress?

C: He seemed younger than me and I wanted to make sure I looked sexy.

M: Hold on, what is sexy to you?

C: Men prefer short colorful dresses . . .

M: What kind of men prefer short colorful dresses?

C: I don't know, every man...

M: As said who?

C: I think I read it in a fashion magazine.

M: What fashion magazine?

C: Not sure or maybe my friend Jennifer told me, I can't remember...

M: Moving forward, what do YOU think is sexy?

C: Well, men want to see some skin, I work out so I want to show my legs, my arms, my cleavage.

M: You want to be as uncovered as possible? Is it what you are telling me?

C: Now you make me think... omg you make me think again.... Does it mean I look cheap? Do I look trashy? What does it mean? So much emotional stuff going on.

M: So what happened to your date?

C: At first the conversation was going well, then we went for a drink and then, not so great.

M: What happened?

C: After the drink, he tried to kiss me, several times in fact, and then he was pushy and tried to touch me. Actually, I now just remember...

M: Remember what?

C: While pushing him away, he said, with that dress what do you expect? Oh my God, I cannot believe I forgot that (she continued), looking down and kind of disappointed. This process is making me think too much and here I was thinking it was going on the yes or no pile. So much analysis, you make me face myself, so hard...

M: This wardrobe contains your life story. Let's continue to see who you are...

C: Really? I guess so...

It kept on going. My next selection was based on style giving me clues of time, such as jackets with epaulettes, translating the 90s so clearly, so boxy and square, mark of my client's youth, when life, right out of college, the first lawyer's job, in the city, on top of the world feeling like a boss, filled with hope and dreams, meeting her prince charming and aiming for this junior partner associate position.

Well, that's what she said when I was asking questions and talking about the process of letting go. By parting away from this fun decade felt to her like killing memories, just like when someone so dear to your heart passes away and by keeping all their belongings feels like they are still around. Same principal here, by hanging on to clothes from the past was a reminder of what good life used to feel like, when everything was possible before a painful divorce, a miscarriage, or a broken heart. Just 90s pieces to anyone from the outer world, yet so precious to her, footprint of once upon a time. So not just clothing after all....

Just like my client, if you want to make a change in your closet, change your style, embrace the current trend, it takes work and time. We are reactive beings, emotional creatures, we respond to instinct.

When buying an article of clothing, getting this accessory or that pair of shoes, it makes you feel a certain way So when in distress, in a down feeling or an urge to just get anything to patch up this negative thought, take a moment. Literally. Stop and think. How does it make you feel? Why do you think you want it? Is it compulsive and well thought? Have you even tried it on? Please try it on. Go in front of the mirror. Stare at yourself in the mirror. Think. Think again. Evaluate, assess, and address its purpose.

If in doubt, just let go, walk away, go home and let this impulse rest. If you are thinking about it tomorrow, there is a possibility you truly want it. But if you forgot all about it? It is your clue to show this desire was only a short moment in time. Just like an investment or buying your dream house, it takes time to put your style together.

The more piled up in your closet, the more confusion in your mind. The more clutter in your wardrobe, the more it is time to re-evaluate what is going on in your life. The way you look right now is telling the world your story so tell your story well.

Clothing is feeling. Style is life. Fashion is emotion.

This is called Personal Branding. Alignment of all your emotions.

BONUS
MATERIAL

Patrice Bisiot Personal Branding Program

As you have seen from the clients we have reviewed in this book, a personal brand is who you are, what you stand for, the values you embrace, and the way in which you express those values.

Personal Branding Is Your Story

The way you tell your story impacts your life entirely. It is the point of connection when you walk into the room. It is crucial in establishing or elevating your career, relationships, sense of self-worth. Your personal brand must highlight your strengths, establish a reputation, build trust, and communicate your message, the uniqueness of You.

Developing a personal brand might seem difficult and overwhelming. This is why from now on, step-by-step, we work together so you can understand the process it takes to build an authentic, personal brand—and amplify your life to the next level.

1. Figure Out Who You Are

In order to build a personal brand that accurately reflects your identity, you first need to know who you are. Be introspective, and create a list of your personal strengths and weaknesses. Get out your journal and answer the following questions:

- In which areas of life do I excel? Where do I struggle?
- What motivates me? What bores me?
- Which activities seem to drain my energy? Which energize me?

- What characteristics have others complimented me on? What characteristics do I admire in others?
- What do other people compliment me on? Where am I self-conscious?
- Which projects do I start and never finish? Which projects does it feel like time has stopped and I never seem to feel tired or overwhelmed?

If you are struggling to answer these questions, ask friends, family, and co-workers how they would describe you. Once you are more aware of the different facets of your personality, you can decide how best to brand them.

Keep in mind, you are not alone. So many people struggle to choose a specific niche because they don't want to limit themselves. Realize your personal brand is your journey. Just like many corporate brands, it will change as your life evolves. The best strategy is to choose a specific area you'd like to focus on and let it expand over time.

2. *Determine What You Want to be Known For*

Your personal brand is more than a reflection of who you are today; it is a roadmap of where you want to go. In addition to understanding your existing skills and competencies, assess your strengths and weaknesses as they relate to whichever area of life you want to break into next.

Take your journal and answer these questions:

- Imagine it is 1 year from today. Write down what you have accomplished in the year. Lost weight? Got fit? Found your great love? New job? New business? Your book was published? Learned a new skill? What did you do with those 12 months?
- Do the same exercise for 5 and 10 years from today. Be very specific on how you used the time to create the life you deserve.
- Go way out and write your eulogy. What do you wish to be remembered for? What kind of person were you? How did your presence on this planet change just one life?

By doing this, you'll uncover the skills and traits which make you distinct, as well as the areas where you need to improve or gain new knowledge in order to advance.

3. *Gap Analysis*

If you have done exercise 1 and 2 VERY thoroughly, you are ready to take the next steps. Now you know who you are, what you represent and where you want to go. It is crucial and much easier to craft your story. By taking your time to answer each question you finally understand YOUR story, the one you need to tell and how to convey it!

This exercise you will use your computer.

Now you have defined who you think you are and where you are going. Go to magazines, websites, social media and other places with images and collect inspirational pictures of the people you see who represent you the most, who you are.

Once you have gathered your images, look closely at your selection. Overall, what is the feel? What have you chosen? Are they chic and trendy? Professional and polished? Hip and urban? Trend setters or trend followers? Do they stand out in the crowd or blend in? Do they have a statement outfit (Steve Jobs black T and jeans) or do they make the outfit have a statement (Cher, Gaga, Bond)?

List everything you see in those images with a common theme. Hair, clothes, posture, expression, location, mood, etc.

Now let's make some conclusions on what you collected. Look at those images, lay them down side by side with the images' collection of yourself. Are there any things in common? Do you see images where photos of yourself are similar in style, posture, clothing as your ideal image? Then you are on the right track!

4. Becoming "You"

Now we know where you are and where you want to go. You understand the point of departure and your destination, your goal, your PURPOSE. Let's review the steps to create the image of the inner you to create the *impact* you want on the world!

- 〈 Closet Assessment:
  - 〈 Hair Assessment:
  - 〈 Lifestyle:
- 〈 Self-Development Evaluation:
- 〈 Body Posture:
- 〈 Body Language:
- 〈 Voice Pitch:

5. Prepare Your Elevator Pitch

You are now building your authentic personal brand.

Remember the moment you walk into the room, it takes a nanosecond to make a life lasting Impact. There is NO second chance, NO re-do. The moment you show up is the only one people will remember. Now you are ready. It is time to craft your elevator pitch—a 30- to 60-second story about who you are.

The exercises above were to create a "visual story" to match your "verbal story." You were aligning both to convey your message clearly. Whether you are going on a first date, networking, attending an informal party or business meeting, simply meeting someone for the first time, or presenting at an event, having an elevator pitch prepared makes it easy to describe succinctly who you are, what you do, and what you offer the world.

You need to create a short, concise, and succinct message to share with the world your authenticity, your core values, and to build trust—stories to tell—sharply framing your attributes in the right light. Keep your elevator pitch brief by focusing on the key points you want to emphasize. This includes your strengths, who you truly are, and your inner self. Time to embrace and display who YOU ARE. Convey clarity, be passionate, and express your purpose.

Mine?

I am a style interventionist.

I help You to build Your Brand.

I apply my skills to guarantee Your "story," aligning Your emotions with Your appearance to insure Your evergreen success.

I guide You to simply understand the psychology of appearance and its Impact.

I am here so You can finally tell the world who You are, to be Brand Ready, to be Image Impact Index Ready.

A Final Note

THE TIME IS THE NEAR PRESENT. The place is in Queens, New York, a special college-prep high school for girls from low-income families. Its mission is to empower young women for careers in science, technology, engineering, and mathematics.

Whenever I can, when I'm in New York, I volunteer my time there as a guest mentor. These hard-working young women are all bright-eyed now...they know they are expected to be trainblazers. But they will soon have to navigate the world and will need all the support they can get.

About the Author

PATRICE BISIOT is an international best-selling author, professional keynote speaker, Branding and Image Consultant. He first discovered his speaking gift at the age of fifteen while standing in front of hundreds of students at a Paris-based Beauty Academy, explaining the principles of clients psychology. Being at the top of his craft was always a priority. Since then, Patrice has motivated thousands of people internationally to build their brand by aligning their emotions and appearance to impact their lives, creating evergreen success.

As a Branding and Image Consultant, Patrice has mentored more than 1,000 clients worldwide to create their vision, mission, and purpose. With his step-by-step Image Impact Index process, he has transformed every single client into a success story!

Patrice's "STYLE INTERVENTION" message has been heralded in influential newspapers, TV and media worldwide.

Patrice is the author of the bestseller *Mind Your Hair,* speaking and coaching globally on the importance of "Beauty from within." His interactive Keynotes, based on his knowledge with years of experience in Hollywood, on the red carpet with celebrities or global leaders, are explaining the mindset of appearance and its impact, initial path to building purposeful personal and professional branding. As a result, his second book *Mind Your Impact, Style Interventionist* is globally distributed.

Originally from Paris, France, Patrice divides his time between the US and Europe, sharing his passion and message across the globe to help one person or crowd at a time, empowering others throughout their journey, to leave a legacy.

Notes & Ideas

PLEASE USE THE NEXT PAGES to jot down ideas, questions, and inspirations as you go through this book, chapter by chapter. Then consult it each time you consider changing your hairstyle, your clothing, or anything representing your personality so you don't repeat your previous thought process. Remember, pen and paper is the only way for your brain to process your thoughts into actions.

When you are done, scan this QR Code so I can answer your questions!

Talk to you soon!

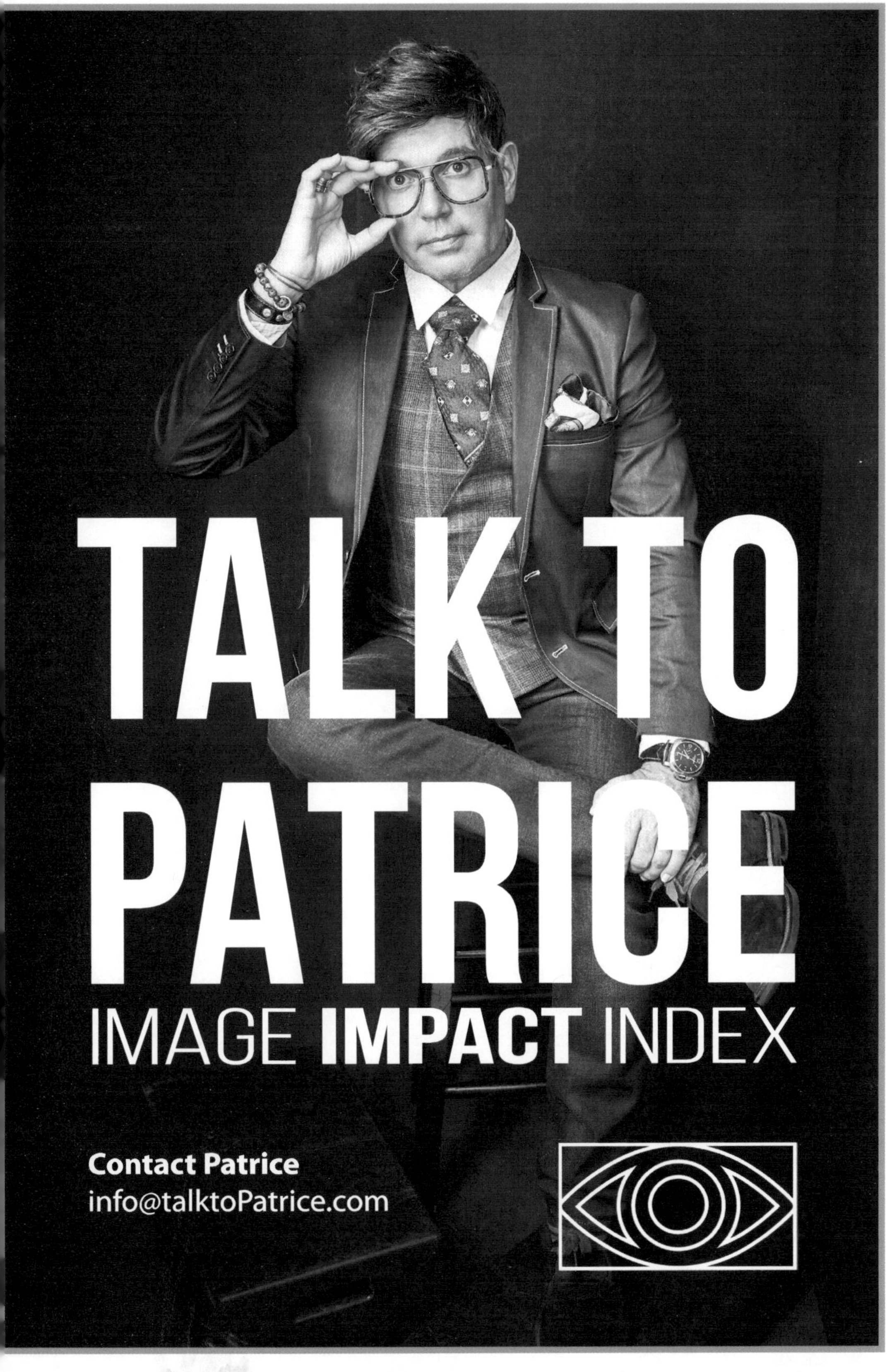
TALK TO
PATRICE
IMAGE IMPACT INDEX
Contact Patrice
info@talktoPatrice.com